ABOVE ALL, *Love*

MY GIFT

I have not much to offer Thee——
No silver, gold, nor fame.
I nothing have but me, you see
A heart to praise Thy name.

No off'ring but a stamm'ring tongue
Two eager hands, but slow.
A willing mind, a ready soul
'Tis weak, and this you know.

My gift so humble, and so weak;
I am so prone to fall.
If Thou canst use it, take it please——
I give to Thee my all!
JENNIFER QUARTELL

ABOVE ALL, *Love*

REFLECTIONS *on* *the* GREATEST COMMANDMENT

JULIE ACKERMAN LINK

DISCOVERY HOUSE

PUBLISHERS

Discovery House Publishers is affiliated with
RBC Ministries, Grand Rapids, MI 49501.

Requests for permission to quote from this book should be directed to:
Permissions Department, Discovery House Publishers,
P.O. Box 3566, Grand Rapids, MI 49501 or contact us by e-mail at
permissionsdept@dhp.org

Scripture quotations are taken from the Holy Bible, New International
Version®. © 1973, 1978, 1984 by Biblica, Inc.™ Used by permission of
Zondervan. All rights reserved worldwide. www.zondervan.com

Above All, Love has been adapted from *The Art of Loving God, Loving God with
All My Heart, Loving God with All My Soul, Loving God with All My Mind,* and
Loving God with All My Strength, © 2003, 2004, 2005, 2006, 2007
by Julie Ackerman Link.

Part of the section titled "The Strength of My Life: Integrity" is adapted
from the introduction, written by Julie Ackerman Link, to *Our Daily Bread:
A Selection of Daily Readings from the Popular Devotional,* © 1997 by Discovery
House Publishers. Used by permission of Discovery House Publishers,
Grand Rapids, MI 49501.

Library of Congress Cataloging-in-Publication Data
Available upon request.

Printed in the United States of America

11 12 13 14 15 / 10 9 8 7 6 5 4 3 2

to Mom and Dad,
whose love for God and for me has been
a constant example of how to love

to Jay,
who demonstrates his love for me
even when I am unlovable

Contents

PART 1: WITH ALL MY HEART

PART 2: WITH ALL MY SOUL

PART 3: WITH ALL MY MIND

PART 4: WITH ALL MY STRENGTH

Introduction

WHEN GOD DESCENDED from heaven in His fiery presence to meet Moses on Mount Sinai, He delivered a document citing ten basic rules for His people to live by. The first and most important was this: "You shall have no other gods before me."

This statement was revolutionary. All other civilizations worshiped many gods. But God's chosen people, the children of Israel, were to establish a nation that would be a light to the world, revealing to all others the joy and peace that come when people live in accord with the design and purpose of our loving Creator, the one true God, who formed us in His own image.

Years later, Moses explained the first commandment. Having no other god but God means loving Him with every aspect of our being—heart, soul, and strength

(Deuteronomy 6:5). Jesus later affirmed this interpretation (Mark 12:30). To love God means having a relationship with Him that is so full and satisfying that it crowds out all competing desires, identifications, thoughts, or actions.

Since the day God delivered the first hand-made edition of the document now called "The Ten Commandments," sculptors, calligraphers, and designers have formed the words into works of art. But God's intent was not that we would shape the words into ornate decorations; instead, He wants the words to shape us. God's law of love is not something to be made into an ornament that adorns ourselves or our buildings; it's to form us into the unique piece of artwork God designed us to be.

> Carve your name on hearts and not on marble.
>
> CHARLES SPURGEON

Loving God is not about creating something beautiful for Him; it's about allowing Him to re-create in us the beauty He originally formed. It's there, and it's waiting to be recognized, restored, and made real.

What Is Love?

I LOVE ART FAIRS. I admire the creativity of the artists, and I enjoy buying unique things. At one art fair, I found a pin that features the faces of three characters from *The Wonderful Wizard of Oz*. Dangling beneath the face of the friendly but Cowardly Lion is a yellow star with the words "Be Brave." Beneath the hollow stare of the Tin Woodman hangs a red heart with the words "Have a Heart." And beneath the mindless expression of the Scarecrow is a turquoise circle with the words "Use Your Brain."

The artist was memorializing L. Frank Baum's children's classic, but I saw the pin as a symbol of what Jews call *Shema*, and what Jesus called the Greatest Commandment.

When Moses addressed a throng of recently freed slaves after leading them out of Egypt following 500 years of captivity, he began with these words:

Hear, O Israel: The LORD our God, the LORD is one. Love the LORD your God with all your heart and with all your soul and with all your strength. (Deuteronomy 6:4–5)

Thousands of years later, Jewish religious leaders asked Jesus, "What is the most important commandment?" He answered them by quoting Moses:

> Love cannot survive if you just give it scraps of yourself, scraps of your time, scraps of your thoughts.
> **MARY O'HARA**

The most important one is this: "Hear, O Israel, the Lord our God, the Lord is one. Love the Lord your God with all your heart and with all your soul and with all your mind and with all your strength." (Mark 12:29–30)

Before the art fair, I had been studying the Greatest Commandment, so I recognized spiritual significance in the pin. In the Tin Woodman who finally feels emotion, I saw a symbol of loving God with my heart. In the Scarecrow who discovers that he can think, I saw a symbol of loving God with my mind. And in the Cowardly Lion who finds courage, I saw a symbol of loving God with my strength.

I bought the pin to wear as a reminder that I'm to love God in all these aspects of my life.

The trouble with the pin, however, as with any symbol, is that its value is limited if we don't understand what it represents. A symbol cannot answer the question: What does it mean to love God with my heart, soul, mind, and strength? Nor can it tell me how to do it.

Everyone admits that love is wonderful and necessary, but no one can agree on what it is.
DIANE ACKERMAN

Years ago in an editorial meeting, one of the writers told of a time when she had admitted to an older, mature Christian that she wasn't sure what it meant to love God. She then described the look of disbelief that she received in return for her confession. That "look" kept her from ever again admitting such a thing—until that moment in our meeting. We then went around the table asking ourselves the question: What does it mean to love God? Even though we all had positions of leadership in our church and other religious organizations, none of us did a very good job of articulating what it means to love God.

The question bothered me so much that I decided I needed to answer it. But before I could answer what it means to love God, I had to ask myself some difficult questions about my own use of the word *love*. How is it that I use the same word to express fondness for art fairs and Mexican food as I do for God? And why is it that my use of the word *love* is often more sincere when I'm referring to the dog who worships me than the God I claim to worship?

What, then, is the meaning of this mysterious four-letter verb/noun that we use to describe everything from the absurd to the sacred, from feelings to actions, from preferences to passions?

Part of the problem is the word itself. The Hebrew Old Testament and the Greek New Testament both have more than one word that is translated love. And my English dictionary lists twenty-one definitions of love. When a single word has so many meanings, it's no wonder we have so much confusion about it.

> The Eskimos had fifty-two names for snow because snow was important to them; there ought to be as many for love.
>
> **MARGARET ATWOOD**

We can easily describe what it feels like to "be loved," but we have trouble translating that into what it means to "be loving." We feel loved when someone wants to be with us, takes the risk of letting us know him or her, takes the time to get to know us, and always does what is in our best interest. Our desire to be on the receiving end of this kind of devotion is always greater than our ability to return it.

To be loved is one of the strongest of all desires. The

need for love is as much a part of God's design for humans as the need for air, water, and food. We can't lead a healthy life without it.

Sadly, humans have managed to thoroughly mess up God's distribution system. One of the ways God passes along His love is through others. Children learn to love by being loved by moms and dads, grandpas and grandmas, aunts and uncles.

A birthday card I bought for my mother was short and simple. It read, "Before I knew anything else, I knew how it felt to be loved. Thanks, Mom. Happy Birthday."

I take for granted the love of my parents, but many people have never known this blessing. My heart breaks when I hear stories about children like Melissa. From as early as she can remember, her parents treated her as if she were less than human. During the day, she was locked in a closet. At mealtime, she was taken outside on a leash and made to eat on the porch. Relatives called her "it." The only emotion Melissa learned to feel was anger, so anger is what she learned to express. At age twelve, she was removed from her abusive family by child protective services, but in every foster family her behavior remained the same—rage and violence—even toward those who truly wanted to help her. As a last resort, she was placed in a Christian residential care center for troubled children. Within a year Melissa's heart began to soften. From people who were kind to her, she learned how to express kindness. Eventually, she turned her life over to God because she had experienced His love through the care and concern of godly counselors and staff. Melissa came to love God and others because God's people loved her.

Those who have grown up in loving homes may be more willing than Melissa to trust love, but they may also be more likely to believe lies.

If we grow up believing the romanticized definition—that being in love means feeling passion— we may not believe those who tell us that loving another human being is difficult work that requires knowledge, skill, and perseverance to go along with emotion. By focusing on the emotion and neglecting the behavior, we make ourselves vulnerable to all kinds of false expressions of love. Imperfect understanding makes us prone to being deceived as well as to being deceptive. So

> Few people know what they mean when they say, "I love you." . . . Well, what does the word love mean? It means total interest. I think the reason very few people really fall in love with anyone is they're not willing to pay the price. The price is you have to adjust yourself to them.
>
> **KATHARINE HEPBURN**

what is the sacred meaning of this word that has been twisted and distorted by overuse and misuse?

The Bible describes love in this familiar New Testament passage:

> Love is patient, love is kind. It does not envy, it does not boast, it is not proud. It is not rude, it is not self-seeking, it is not easily angered, it keeps no record of wrongs. Love does not delight in evil but rejoices with the truth. It always protects, always trusts, always hopes, always perseveres.
> (1 Corinthians 13:4–7)

Genuine love seeks the highest good for someone other than self. God's love is perfect because He seeks the highest good for all creation. Every human being longs to receive this kind of love, but none of us can give it unless we first receive it from God. The only place to experience genuine love is in a relationship with the One whose very being defines love. Not only is God the perfect *example* of love, He *is* love, and apart from His love for us none of us could love or be loved (1 John 4:19).

> In real love, you want the other person's good. In romantic love, you want the other person.
> MARGARET ANDERSON

God Is Love

WHY IS THERE SO MUCH HATRED?

ON OCTOBER 8, 2002, curators at New York's Metropolitan Museum of Art mourned the fall of Adam, a tragedy of such magnitude that it brought them to their knees. But they were not repenting of the sin that started in the Garden of Eden with the fall of the first Adam. They were lamenting the plunge of a priceless fifteenth-century sculpture from its pedestal, and they were on their knees picking up the fragments.

When the statue fell, it didn't break into nice neat pieces. The arms, legs, and head were separated from the torso in such a way that they could not easily be pieced and glued back together. According to the restorer, part of Adam was "pulverized." Experts predicted that it would take two years to put Adam together again, but they promised that he would be almost as good as new by the time he was returned to public view.

Imagine having the dust and particles of Adam given to you and being told to put him back together again. That would be a small example of what we attempt to do whenever we try to "restore" ourselves from the effects of the Fall.

Like the statue, the original Adam and everyone after him have been pulverized by sin. We did not break into pieces that can be easily identified as emotions, personality, mind, and body. We lie in a pile of dust and broken body parts on the floor of creation. And we have only one hope for wholeness—the One who created us is the only One with the knowledge and skill to put us back together.

> In him all things hold together.
> COLOSSIANS 1:17

In a letter to Christians living in Asia Minor (now Turkey), the apostle Paul disclosed the bonding agent that Jesus uses to restore us to our original glory:

> Therefore, as God's chosen people, holy and dearly loved, clothe yourselves with compassion, kindness, humility, gentleness and patience. Bear with each other and forgive whatever grievances you may have against one another. Forgive as the Lord forgave you. And over all these virtues put on love, which binds them all together in perfect unity. (Colossians 3:12–14)

In another letter, this one to Christians living in Corinth, Paul wrote "Love never fails" (1 Corinthians 13:8).

If that is true, why did love fail to keep sin from entering the Garden of Eden? If love never fails, where does all the hate come from? What are the answers to the questions so many people keep asking when terrible things happen: How can God be good and yet allow so much evil? How can He be all-powerful and yet do nothing to stop all the suffering? How can He be the full expression of love and yet tolerate so much hatred?

When we consider the options available, however, we realize that God made the most loving choice of all when He gave us freedom, even though this freedom includes the option to reject Him and thus opens the door to evil.

For love to exist, rejection must be an option, for love requires that choice be involved. In fact, it is our freedom to reject God that proves how much He really does love us. A deity who forced himself on us would be a rapist, not a lover. A deity who stood over us with a clenched fist would be a tyrant, not a loving father. And a deity who constrained us to behave a certain way would be a slave driver, not a savior.

In the ultimate act of self-sacrifice, God paid far more for us than we are worth. Yet instead of using force to hold us, He relies on the splendor of His love to attract us. In extravagant expressions of truth, goodness, and beauty, He woos us. He longs for us to desire Him, not just His gifts. But He waits for us to choose Him.

Love cannot be forced, love cannot be coaxed and teased. It comes out of Heaven, unasked and unsought.

PEARL BUCK

First Love

BEGINNING WITH ADAM AND EVE, God has been making it His priority to establish a relationship with the people He created—first one couple, then one family, then one nation, and now the world. To reconcile the world to Himself and bring everyone into His family, He proved His love by sending His Son.

> This is how God showed his love among us: He sent his one and only Son into the world that we might live through him. (1 John 4:9; see also 2 Corinthians 5:18–19)

In doing so, God expressed His love with His heart, soul, mind, and strength. This means that God asks of us only what He first demonstrated to us!

We learn to love God by discovering how He loves us.

GOD LOVES US WITH HIS HEART—
He Wants a Relationship with Us

We often misunderstand the role of feelings, emotion, and desire in regard to love. Some of us exaggerate their importance while others disregard them due to the confusion and complexity they add to relationships. But all three are a legitimate part of love, and God's love for us involves all three.

The LORD your God is with you, he is mighty to save. He will take great delight in you, he will quiet you with his love, he will rejoice over you with singing.
ZEPHANIAH 3:17

Moses assures us that God feels compassion for us and is slow to become angry (Exodus 34:6). The prophet Zephaniah said that God "delights" in us (3:17). And Jesus, at the last Passover meal, prayed, "Father, I want those you have given me to be with me where I am" (John 17:24).

God's love involves the way He feels about us, not just the way He acts toward us.

Try to recall your first love. Think about how it felt to learn that someone you liked also liked you and found you delightful and desirable?

Imagine that someone being God!

23

GOD LOVES US WITH HIS SOUL—
He Reveals Himself to Us

Only the last book of the Bible is titled "Revelation," but all of Scripture *is* revelation. All sixty-six books are a record of God's many attempts to let Himself be known by those He created. (See Amos 4:13; Isaiah 43:10.)

In addition, creation itself is an act of revelation. We know people by what they create. Poets, songwriters, and storytellers reveal something of themselves in their art. The same is true of God.

And finally, God sent Jesus—deity dressed in flesh—so that He could introduce Himself on our level. Then Jesus made this stunning statement to His disciples: "The knowledge of the secrets of the kingdom of heaven has been given to you," (Matthew 13:11).

Think about how special you feel when someone trusts you enough to tell you his or her secrets.

Imagine that someone being God!

GOD LOVES US WITH HIS MIND—
He Knows What We Need

No loving parent expects a toddler to mow the lawn, repair the car, or fix meals. Likewise, God does not expect His children to perform tasks beyond their ability. Because He made us, He knows our limitations.

> As a father has compassion on his children, so the LORD has compassion on those who fear him; for he knows how we are formed, he remembers that we are dust. (Psalm 103:13–14)

We sometimes think that a loving relationship with God begins when we figure out what He wants us to do for Him, but that's not true; it begins when we realize everything He wants to do for us.

The pieces of themselves that mothers and fathers give away day after day might seem wasted. But they are life's daily doses of love wrapped in persistence and patience.

SUSAN LENZKES

Imagine a hungry orphan in a war-torn country having someone in a position of world leadership visit her impoverished village, kneel before her, look into her eyes, and say, "I'd like to take you home with me and make you part of my family. Do you want to come?" That's what God wants to do for each of us. Perhaps you've been in a difficult situation with no obvious way out when someone came alongside you and said, "You're having a hard time, aren't you? Will you let me help you?"

Imagine that someone being God!

GOD LOVES US WITH HIS STRENGTH— *He Gives Us What Is Good*

"Don't take candy from strangers." Behind this timeless

warning is this stark truth: evil, to get what it wants, disguises itself as good. Like pedophiles who present themselves as kind and generous, Satan masquerades as the one giving out all the goodies. But the "gifts" of Satan are all counterfeits. They lead to futility, despair, and uselessness. The gifts of God, on the other hand, lead to purpose, meaning, and fruitfulness (James 1:16–18).

Loving parents do not indulge a child's every craving, but they eagerly and joyfully supply every need. Parents give many additional gifts as well, not to bribe children or lure them for some selfish purpose, but because they love to see their children happy.

Being loved means having someone know us so well and care about us so much that he uses all his strength to give us what is good and do what is best for us even before we ask, even when we don't know what it is.

Imagine that someone being God!

AS PERFECT AS GOD'S LOVE IS, it will not satisfy us if we simply receive it. To

> Love has nothing to do with what you are expecting to get—only what you are expecting to give—which is everything. What you will receive in return varies. But it really has no connection with what you give. You give because you love and cannot help giving. If you are very lucky, you may be loved back. That is delicious, but it does not necessarily happen.
>
> **KATHARINE HEPBURN**

be complete, love must flow in two directions. It must be received *and* reciprocated. Therefore, God's call "of" love is paired with His command "to" love.

Love is not a reservoir that we fill up and save for later use. It's a river that flows from God to us and back to God again through our love for other people. Jesus said, "A new command I give you: Love one another. As I have loved you, so you must love one another. By this all men will know that you are my disciples, if you love one another" (John 13:34–35).

Our willingness to love others affects our ability to feel loved. If we refuse to love, eventually we will feel unloved. God's people drifted away from Him not because He stopped loving them, but because they stopped "feeling loved" when they started loving God's gifts more than they loved the Giver.

The desire to be loved is not wrong. God Himself wants to be loved, so much so that He made it the most important commandment, as the *Shema* states and as Jesus confirmed.

The greatest adversary of love to God is not his enemies but his gifts. And the most deadly appetites are not for the poison of evil, but for the simple pleasures of earth. For when these replace an appetite for God himself, the idolatry is scarcely recognizable, and almost incurable.
JOHN PIPER

God did not leave us in the dark as to what it means to

love Him; nor does He make us guess how He wants to be loved. In fact, He didn't just tell us, He showed us! God wants us to love Him in the same way He loves us—with every desire and feeling, with every aspect of our being, with every thought, and with everything we do.

WITH ALL MY *Heart*

Does It Matter What I Want?

STANDING ON THE EASTERN SIDE of the Jordan River, not far from where Moses stood to view the Promised Land, I gazed across the Jordan Valley and tried to imagine standing alongside the ancient Israelites, seeing for the first time the land that God referred to as "flowing with milk and honey."

"Did this look a lot different when the Israelites got here?" I asked our guide.

I didn't want my disappointment to show, but I was expecting something dramatic, a stunning view that would make me gasp at its beauty and its startling contrast to the wilderness landscape on the eastern side of the Jordan Valley.

"No," she answered. "This is how it has looked for thousands of years."

I searched my mind for an explanation that would reconcile what I was expecting to see with what I was actually seeing. The other side of the Jordan looked much the same as where I was standing.

Later I asked the question in a different way. "What do you think the Israelites saw when they got here?"

Our guide quickly answered, "The biggest oasis on the face of the whole earth," referring to what is now the city of Jericho.

I had ridden across the barren landscape in the luxury of an air-conditioned tourist bus stocked with cold bottled water. To me, an oasis was nothing spectacular. The Israelites had spent forty years trekking around a hot, dusty desert. To them, the sprawling patch of pale green they could see in the hazy distance indicated the presence of water—an abundant supply of life-sustaining water.

To see the beauty of the Promised Land requires a change in perspective. It has to be viewed through the eyes of one who is tired and thirsty and who recognizes it as the place chosen by God to raise His family and to nurture them in truth and trust.

Before visiting Israel, I pictured the Holy Land as drab and dust-covered. Childhood Bible lessons in fuzzy flannelgraph left the impression that the color palette of Bible lands ranged from olive green to desert brown.

But after spending time in Israel, I see it differently. Every picture is now beautiful. What makes Israel lovely is not the predominance of brilliant colors, but finding spots of color in so many unexpected places.

The psalmist David wrote, "Taste and see that the LORD is good" (Psalm 34:8). The milk and honey of God's goodness are often found in unexpected places, sometimes even dry, difficult places. But once we experience it, we long for more, and we lose our desire for all lesser substitutes.

> That we ought to love Him we are never in doubt, but whether we do love Him, we may well begin to question. A deep yearning in our innermost being "to know Him more clearly, love Him more dearly and follow Him more nearly" is probably all to which we dare lay claim.
>
> HELEN ROSEVEARE

EVE'S FIRST ACT OF WRONGDOING started with a wrong desire. Sin started growing when Eve wanted something God didn't want her to have. This may explain why the curse on Eve involves desire. According to Genesis, her "desire" will be for her husband (3:16). Interpreting this from the perspective of twentieth-century western middle-class culture, some have concluded that this means women will desire man's authority. But when we look at it in light of male-female relationships throughout history and across cultures, a different picture emerges.

In many cultures, women remain voluntarily subservient (not to be mistaken with submissive) to men because they need a man to protect them and take care of them. Even western women find this idea appealing, like the well-educated young woman who was re-thinking the western practice of dating and marriage. "Forget this 'love is all we need' stuff," she commented. "I want security."

Some men exploit a woman's need for protection and her desire for security, and they use it to rule over her in ways that God never intended.

Some women want a man—any man—at any cost. But not all males are good men, and women who desire a man more than they desire God are courting trouble for themselves and for their offspring.

Desire itself is not bad; it's part of our emotional makeup that God established at creation. Desire works in conjunction with feelings and emotions to stimulate, energize, and enable us to experience life to the fullest. Our own feelings and desires help us understand the part of God's character that is emotional. When desire is satisfied, we feel good, at least temporarily; when it's not, we feel bad. To enjoy good feelings that are not subject to changing circumstances, we need to align our desires with God's. This is where Eve went wrong.

Eve allowed Satan to seduce her, and the seed he planted within her was the desire for knowledge that God didn't want her to have. At Satan's prompting, Eve began doubting God's love for her (the starting place of much sin). She began questioning whether God had her best interests or His own in mind when He set limits on the food she could eat and the knowledge she could have. Sin conceived gave birth to death, and thus began the downward plunge.

Satan is no creative genius, but he's an expert at creating doubt. Since his initial success with Eve, he's been perfecting his skill by practicing on all her offspring. The lie that Satan has used successfully throughout history is that God is the enemy, that He is stingy, and that He will keep us from getting what we need, want, and deserve. Satan takes advantage of our need for love by making us feel as if God's love is insufficient. Then he slithers in to tempt us with tasty counterfeits.

Satan would have us believe that we have no control over our feelings, desires, and emotions—that they come to us uninvited and that we are powerless to change them or make them leave. As usual, he is partly right. They do come to us uninvited, and we have no power to change them. But God does! And He is eager to change our desires and empower us to choose what is good . . . but only if we will ask.

> Flee the evil desires of youth, and pursue righteousness, faith, love and peace, along with those who call on the Lord out of a pure heart.
>
> 2 TIMOTHY 2:22

My Desire

WHY DO I WANT WHAT I SHOULDN'T HAVE?

Eat what you want and lose weight. Promises like this clutter the covers of women's magazines month after month, and women want to believe them. We want to believe that there is an easy, painless way to have the perfect body. Give us a plan, and we will follow it—at least for a day or two, maybe even a week.

But if these diets work so well, why do we need a new one every month in every magazine? And why do so many of us continue our battle of the bulge year after year?

The truth is, the only way to eat what we want and lose weight is to want what causes weight loss. In other words, our desires have to change before diets will work. The desire to be thin is not enough; we must also desire what is good for us—nutritious foods and plenty of exercise.

This is unwelcome information. We don't want to change

our desires; we want different results from having our desires satisfied!

Health officials have estimated that more than 60 percent of Americans are overweight, and a Google search for "weight loss" turned up 126 million results.

Starvation is not our problem. Hunger is.

The desire to feel satisfied has led us to believe that feeling hunger is bad, so we look for eating programs that guarantee weight loss without nagging hunger pangs or rude growling sounds. But the problem with hunger is that we perceive it wrongly and use it inappropriately. We perceive hunger wrongly when we see it as an enemy rather than an ally. God created it for a purpose and uses it for our good. Hunger keeps us alive—both physically and spiritually:

We are hungry for something, but it's not food. Even when we stuff our stomachs, we remain emotionally starved.

> He humbled you, causing you to hunger and then feeding you with manna, which neither you nor your fathers had known, to teach you that man does not live on bread alone but on every word that comes from the mouth of the LORD. (Deuteronomy 8:3)

We use hunger wrongly when we try to satisfy it apart from God. Hunger is meant to remind us of our need for God, and having hunger satisfied is meant to remind us to be grateful: "When you have eaten and are satisfied, praise the LORD your God for the good land he has given you" (Deuteronomy 8:10). But in the twisted economy of sin, food is thought of as something we have earned—a reward for good behavior or hard work, rather than an indication of God's love and care for creation—and hunger is thought of as evidence that God can't or won't satisfy us.

> The true mortification of our carnal nature is not a simple matter of denial and discipline. It is an internal, spiritual matter of finding more contentment in Christ than in food.
>
> JOHN PIPER

Jesus raised the subject of hunger to a new level in His Sermon on the Mount when He used it as a metaphor to explain that it is good to hunger and thirst for righteousness. Those who do, He said, "will be filled" (Matthew 5:6).

Sadly, righteousness seldom makes it to the top of our "most wanted" list, which explains why we so seldom feel as if we are filled. When we fail to distinguish between spiritual hunger and physical hunger, we end up using food to satisfy feelings of emptiness that only God can fill.

The desire to eat when we're hungry is good because

food sustains life. The desire to eat when we're not hungry is bad because food then replaces life.

"Food is killing us in so many ways," said Amy Wilensky, author of *The Weight of It*, in an interview on the Diane Rehm radio program. Using food as the method of choice, women are committing slow suicide with one of two extremes. By either stuffing or starving ourselves, we use the food that God gives to sustain life in ways that actually take our lives instead. What God intended to make us strong makes us weak when used inappropriately—too much, too little, too sweet, too fat. Each of these springs from desire gone awry. What God meant for good, we use for harm.

> Man finds it hard to get what he wants because he does not want the best; God finds it hard to give because He would give the best, and man will not take it.
>
> GEORGE MACDONALD

Clearly, our desires are in disarray. Not only do we want to enjoy the taste of food, we want to eat as much as we want of whatever we want whenever we feel like it. Not only do we want to feel the satisfaction of a full stomach, we want never to feel hunger and never to be fat.

Popular media perpetuate the mistaken notion that being thin will make us desirable, and that by making ourselves desirable we'll be truly loved. Failing to identify the lie, many Christians join those who are using food and exercise to achieve not only physical perfection but also emotional satisfaction.

But it doesn't work. Our desires lead us astray.

FAULTY SOLUTIONS CAUSE MORE PROBLEMS

Food is just one example of the many things we use inappropriately to satisfy our emotional hunger. When we try to satisfy emotional needs in physical ways we end up feeling bad about ourselves, and so the self-destructive cycle continues.

A friend of mine often quotes a marketing expert who claims that people are motivated by two basic desires: to gain pleasure and to avoid pain. Judging from the spam in my e-mail box, she is right. The products most frequently promoted involve one of the two—usually in the form of pills to enhance sexual pleasure or to eliminate physical or psychological pain.

> There is only one big thing—desire. And before it, when it is big, all is little.
> WILLA CATHER

If you've ever been curious as to why competing drug stores are located on three corners of so many intersections, stop and think about what they are really selling. Products that promise to reduce pain or to increase pleasure are in high demand. When we're in pain, we want relief, and we want it fast. If we are not in pain, we want pleasure, and we want it without consequence or obligation.

Desire is not known for its patience. When we want something—whether pleasure or relief—we want it in a way that is fast, inexpensive, and without complications. We'd rather try every empty promise than admit that we need to change our desire. Desire does not want to be told that it can be satisfied only by changing. Desire wants satisfaction, not a morality lesson.

The idea that we have to want what is good for us goes against everything desire tells us. And the notion that every desire deserves to be satisfied is dangerous both physically and emotionally. When carried over to our spiritual lives, it's even more dangerous because it infects our interpretation of Scripture and our understanding of God.

Passages like Psalm 37:4 are especially vulnerable to sabotage: "Delight yourself in the LORD and he will give you the desires of your heart." To me, this could sound like an invitation to order every book on my Amazon.com wish list. However, the introductory phrase of the verse makes the meaning quite different. The promise only "works" when I desire the delight of the Lord.

When people misread and misuse Scripture they end up blaming God for failing to keep a promise He never made.

Even though I am well aware of this danger, many of my

prayers still sound like this: "Lord, I delight in you. Now can I have what I want? I'd like to be healthy, ageless, and thin. That's not too much to ask, is it?"

THE WAR OF WANTS

Our desires are at war within us. But this is not news. We've been struggling with desires gone awry since Eve's encounter with the serpent in Eden.

Many years later, the apostle Paul acknowledged his own struggle when he wrote to Christians living in Rome:

> When I want to do good, evil is right there with me. For in my inner being I delight in God's law; but I see another law at work in the members of my body, waging war against the law of my mind and making me a prisoner of the law of sin at work within my members. What a wretched man I am! Who will rescue me from this body of death? Thanks be to God—through Jesus Christ our Lord! (Romans 7:21–25)

Like Paul, I too have a war raging between my head and

my heart. Even when I want to do something good, my mind comes up with reasons for not doing it. And even when I desire something good, my mind suggests ungodly shortcuts for acquiring it that are bad for others as well as myself.

I desire . . .

○ to be well thought of (so I say flattering things to people I do not think well of).

○ to be beautiful (so I buy clothes, makeup, and other products to hide my imperfections).

○ to be smart (so I buy books I don't have time to read).

○ to be organized (so I buy notebooks, gadgets, and filing systems that just give me more places to lose things).

○ to be right (so I learn to use words in convincing, but not always kind, ways).

Whenever the desire to achieve something is stronger than the desire to achieve it in God's way, in God's time, and for God's purpose, conflict and chaos result:

> What causes fights and quarrels among you?
> Don't they come from your desires that battle
> within you? You want something but don't get
> it. You kill and covet, but you cannot have what
> you want. You quarrel and fight. You do not have,

because you do not ask God. When you ask,
you do not receive, because you ask with wrong
motives, that you may spend what you get on
your pleasures. (James 4:1–3)

In a Bible study based on the ideas in this book, the
women in my group were answering the question, "What (or
who) is your biggest frustration?" Surprisingly, we all gave
pretty much the same answer: ourselves. For one, it was her
impatience with her children; for another, it was her inability
to lose weight; for another, it was her inability to say no to
speaking invitations; for another, it was her propensity to
disappoint her parents.

Frankly, I was surprised by the responses. I expected
to be the only one whose biggest enemy is myself. My
biggest frustration is my inability to bring order to my life.
This problem manifested itself during childhood but didn't
become debilitating until I went off to college and left
behind the parents who had maintained structure for me.

I considered this problem to be an annoying weakness
until a well-meaning retreat speaker (one who evidently does
not struggle with this area of ineptitude) suggested that it
may instead be a spiritual defect. Speaking to a group of
college students, she asked this probing question: "When
people look inside your car or closet, do they see any

evidence that you believe in a God who brings order out of chaos?"

The truth is, if it depended on me, no one would have reason to conclude that I believe in, am acquainted with, or, much less, am made in the image of a God who brings order out of chaos. Her question has caused me much guilt and anxiety. The guilt comes from the belief that God hates my disorderly ways. The anxiety comes from the fear that maybe He also hates me.

In trying to reconcile my fears and feelings with the truth I've learned about God, I discovered two points of view.

Some people say that I just need to try harder. God wants me to be neat and orderly, so if I want it badly enough I will be. So I try binge cleaning. When I get everything in place I feel good about myself. But only for a while. Within hours the mess is back. Like Pigpen in the *Peanuts* comic strip, I am followed by a cloud of debris.

Others say that being messy is part of being creative and I should just accept myself. God made me this way, so I might as well stop trying to be orderly. So I begin rationalizing that being messy is just an innocuous character trait, not an insidious defect. And I feel better about myself.

But only for a while. I am soon reminded why being messy is not a good way to live—disorder makes life difficult!

So the tension mounts. If I follow the first advice, I'm in danger of becoming like the Pharisees, who led perfectly ordered lives but kept the filth of greed and pride in their hearts. If I follow the second advice, I'm in danger of becoming like the pagans, who led undisciplined lives because they failed to make any distinction between clean and unclean.

As I've struggled to reconcile these opposing options and come to terms with my inadequacy, I've been relieved to discover a third alternative. More important than keeping a clean car or closet is to have a clean heart. Jesus put it this way: "First clean the inside . . . and then the outside also will be clean" (Matthew 23:26).

> Desire is a restless activity, a yearning for something one craves but does not possess. Love, even though it is passionate, has within it an element of repose, of satisfaction, of joy that comes from delight in the presence of the beloved.
> **ROBERT LOUIS WILKEN**

The important question is not "What does the content of my car or closet say to the world about God?" but "What does the content of my heart say to God about me?"

When the first question is more important than the second, I am violating the first commandment, for the thing that frustrates me the most indicates my highest desire, and my highest desire indicates what I worship. On most days, my highest desire is for order, not for God.

 ## God's Top Ten List

What makes me feel good tells me a lot about myself—and sometimes even about what I worship. Do I feel good when everything is in order? Then maybe I worship order. Do I feel good when I have approval, comfort, or sensual pleasure? Then I probably worship those things.

C. D. BAKER

The Bible doesn't give a reason as to why the Ten Commandments are given in the order they are, but it's interesting to note that the tenth commandment correlates to the first sin—desire: You shall not want what isn't yours.

From an earthly standpoint (i.e., looking up from our perspective rather than down from God's), it makes sense to consider the Ten Commandments in reverse order, kind of like a David Letterman Top Ten List, giving first consideration to commandment number ten. After all, if we don't covet, we will pretty much eliminate all of our reasons to lie, steal, or commit adultery.

Even the popular psalm of David, known for its comfort in times of loss, gives prominence to the subject of covetousness by reminding us, first of all, that those who follow the Good Shepherd have no reason to covet: "The LORD is my shepherd, I shall not be in want" (Psalm 23:1), or, as the Jewish Bible translates it, "I lack nothing."

I don't always feel as if this is true, however. My emotions keep telling me that God is withholding something good or trying to trick me into settling for something inferior.

Nevertheless, I know that I ought to want God's will. So I pray, "Lord, I want to want your will. I want to want what you desire. I know this falls short of where I ought to be, but is it anything you can work with?"

Thankfully it is, and He does.

God's Desire

THE LORD IS MY SHEPHERD, the psalmist wrote, I lack nothing. These words begin one of the best-loved passages of Scripture. We quote them to assure one another of God's presence and provision. We repeat them to remind ourselves that we have all we need. Yet still we want more. Being the shepherd of such a restless, dissatisfied flock is no easy job. We humans are like daylight savings time: either springing ahead or falling behind. We covet both the past and the future and disregard the only time we have: today.

We stand on tiptoes trying to see where God is taking us instead of trusting Him to get us there. When we are in the shadow, we assume that we are under a thundercloud rather than in the shelter of God's wings. When we are in the sunlight, we complain that it's too hot or we worry that it won't last. When the wind of trouble starts to howl, we hold on so it can't blow us away rather than let go so it can lift us up.

The birds that nest in the bush outside my office window demonstrate more faith than I do. They do not covet any more time than God gives them. They follow God's rhythm and never miss a beat. They don't debate whether it's time to fly or rest. They don't try to repeat yesterday or change tomorrow. They accept each day as a gift and use it to do what needs to be done: find food, build nests, make music, mate, and prepare their offspring to take their place.

Jesus said that we shouldn't borrow trouble from the past or the future because each day has enough of its own (Matthew 6:34), but my fear of losing what I have, or not getting what I want, keeps me hanging on to what I should release and thus failing to receive what God wants me to have.

I wish it were easy to release the past and relinquish the future. I wish I could accept what comes from God's hand each day as a carefully chosen gift. When the gift is stillness, I wish I would wait in quiet contentment and trust that God will not leave me stranded, that the same Spirit Who got me to a certain place will take me to the next place at God's proper time. When the gift is wind, I wish that I would catch it and soar to the next place God has chosen.

Before heading to Gethsemane, Jesus prayed,

> "Father, I want those you have given me to be
> with me where I am, and to see my glory, the
> glory you have given me because you loved me
> before the creation of the world." (John 17:24)

My highest good comes only when my highest desire is for all of God, not for select morsels on a religious buffet table.

Before we can love God so unreservedly, we need to trust that God wants what is good for us and to be assured that God's highest desire is our highest good.

The apostle Paul assures us that God cares about our emotional well-being when he refers to Him as "the Father of compassion and the God of all comfort" (2 Corinthians 1:3–7).

But God doesn't simply want to mitigate our suffering; He wants to infuse our lives with joy. In fact, enjoyment was built into His perfect plan for creation.

GOD WANTS US TO ENJOY WORK AND REST

Work was part of creation before the fall. It is a blessing, not a curse, and God's desire for each of us is to have meaningful work that matches our gifts and abilities and makes an important contribution to the world:

When God gives any man wealth and possessions, and enables him to enjoy them, to accept his lot and be happy in his work—this is a gift of God. (Ecclesiastes 5:19)

[M]y chosen ones will long enjoy the works of their hands.
ISAIAH 65:22

God also wants us to rest. Even though work is good, it has an inherent danger. The results and rewards of work can make us feel as if our work is more important than God's. God ordained a Sabbath day of rest to remind us that we are dependent on His work, not vice versa.

[A]nyone who enters God's rest also rests from his own work, just as God did from his. Let us, therefore, make every effort to enter that rest, so that no one will fall by following their example of disobedience. (Hebrews 4:10–11)

Many have come to think of rest as just another restriction imposed by a demanding God. But rest is a gift from a loving Father who knows and wants what is good for all His children.

GOD WANTS US TO ENJOY ONE ANOTHER

God created Eve so that Adam would have a companion.

Alone, we are incomplete. To live fully and completely, we need to be engaged in peaceful, harmonious relationships with others and with Him.

Due to human weaknesses such as selfishness and pride, however, we often break the peace. So God's instructions include guidelines not only for *maintaining* peace but also for *restoring* peace.

1. *Be quick to listen, slow to speak, and slow to become angry*, for anger "does not bring about the righteous life that God desires" (James 1:20).

2. *Be forgiving.* "Bear with each other and forgive whatever grievances you may have against one another. Forgive as the Lord forgave you" (Colossians 3:13).

3. *Be imitators of God.* "[A]s dearly loved children . . . live a life of love, just as Christ loved us and gave himself up for us as a fragrant offering and sacrifice to God" (Ephesians 5:1–2).

4. *Be ministers of reconciliation.* When we follow the first three guidelines, the fourth is the inevitable outcome. Being quick to listen, slow to speak, slow to become angry, and willing to forgive makes us an imitator of God. And being an imitator of God, we will be ministers of reconciliation.

> All this is from God, who reconciled us to
> himself through Christ and gave us the ministry

of reconciliation: that God was reconciling the world to himself in Christ, not counting men's sins against them. And he has committed to us the message of reconciliation" (2 Corinthians 5:18–19).

In his book *The Return of the Prodigal Son*, author Henri Nouwen suggests that all Christians, at some point in their walk of faith, are represented by each of the three main characters in Christ's parable of the prodigal son. At times we are the wayward child in need of repentance and forgiveness; at other times we are the big brother who wants to hold on to resentment and withhold forgiveness. But if we mature in faith, we become like the father, whose highest desire is to have all his children reconciled.

Lord, grant me the courage to confess my faults to those I've offended and the grace to accept the confessions of those who have offended me. May I become a true minister of reconciliation by using all my strength to bless the world on your behalf.

Nouwen ended the book with these words: "As I look at my own aging hands, I know that they have been given to me to stretch out to all who suffer, to rest upon the shoulders of all who come, and to offer the blessing that emerges from the immensity of God's love."

As we consider the role we are playing in our family stories, we should ask ourselves: Do I need the courage to repent and seek forgiveness? Or do I need the compassion to extend forgiveness? How can I be God's minister of reconciliation?

GOD WANTS US TO ENJOY HIM

The Westminster Catechism states that the chief and highest end for all people "is to glorify God, and fully to enjoy him forever."

This goes against the thinking of those who believe that God is a spoil sport who wants to squelch everything that is fun by arbitrarily labeling it "sin." On the contrary, over and over in Scripture, God says things like this:

> [I]n the presence of the LORD your God, you
> and your families shall eat and shall rejoice
> in everything you have put your hand to,
> because the LORD your God has blessed you.
> (Deuteronomy 12:7)

The prophet Habakkuk wrote, "I will rejoice in the LORD, I will be joyful in God my Savior" (3:18).

Here are a few of the many ways we can enjoy God:

1. *In seeking Him.* People sometimes grumble because God doesn't make His presence more obvious. They complain that God is too difficult to find, too distant. But God knows

that there is little excitement in finding something we've not had to look for. In fact, it seems to be part of our nature to enjoy finding things. Who can deny the thrill of finding something that has been lost or hidden? As children, we played games of hide-and-seek. At Christmas we wrap presents and at Easter we hide eggs. And Jesus compared the kingdom of heaven to a treasure hidden in a field (Matthew 13:44), and said that He came "to seek and to save what was lost" (Luke 19:10).

God could make His presence more evident if He wanted to. He did in fact do so among the ancient Israelites. But they complained about that. When God delivered the Ten Commandments, His presence was accompanied by thunder, lightning, and smoke. The people were so terrified that they said to Moses, "Speak to us yourself and we will listen. But do not have God speak to us or we will die" (Exodus 20:19).

> Praise the LORD. Blessed is the man who fears the LORD, who finds great delight in his commands.
>
> PSALM 112:1

It seems as if God can't win. People grumble that He is either too far or too close; too uninvolved or too imposing. We accuse God of being difficult to please, but a more accurate conclusion is that *we* are difficult to please.

However, when God seems to be in hiding, we can be confident that He wants to be found; and when God seems to be hounding us, we can be assured that He wants only what is good for us.

2. *In celebrating His goodness.* God established feasts and celebrations as part of the yearly calendar. He mandated seven major holidays, some lasting as long as a week, and three of them were to be celebrated in one giant gathering in Jerusalem.

Like rest, worship was not a duty demanded by a needy god, but a delight planned by a loving and giving God. At intervals throughout the year, all the people stopped their routines and had a party to remember and celebrate all that God had done for them.

Ungrateful people are unhappy people. The opposite is also true. The happiest people are those who are the most grateful for what they have— regardless of how little or how much.

No one ever had an odder guru . . . but I started following his advice by mouthing rote thank-you's to the air, and right off, I discovered something. There was an entire aspect to my life that I had been blind to—the small, good things that came in abundance.

MARY KARR

3. *In following His commands.* According to Oswald Chambers, "God never threatens; the devil never warns." We sometimes use the words *threat* and *warning* interchangeably, but there is an important distinction. Threats are used to get people to do what is in *our* best interest. Warnings are issued to get people to do what is in

their best interest. In other words, threats are an attempt to preserve power by controlling people, whereas warnings are an effort to protect people by keeping them from danger.

"A warning is a great arresting statement of God's, inspired by His love and patience," wrote Chambers. Satan would like us to think of God's loving warnings as mean-spirited threats, but he is wrong, and we are wise to remember the many commands of God that are coupled with phrases like "that it will go well with you" (e.g., Deuteronomy 4:40; 12:28).

In loving relationships, people warn one another of the inevitable consequences of foolish behavior. In unhealthy relationships, people threaten one another with punishment if they fail to live up to unreasonable demands.

As we interact with others, it's good to consider the nature of our counsel and commands. Are we like Satan, using ultimatums to preserve our own well being, or like God, issuing warnings to preserve the well being of others?

God knows us so well that He can foresee the results of our behavior. He also knows that much of what we think will make us happy will bring misery instead, so He gives guidance in the form of warnings to help us avoid the grief that results from bad choices. When we realize this, we will delight in God's commands.

Life Hurts

WHAT CAN I DO WITH THE PAIN?

AT FIVE YEARS OF AGE I began to believe that people who are strong refuse to feel pain. It started when my uncle chose to take his own life.

One of the laws of physics says that for every action there is an equal and opposite reaction. That was true of my uncle's single gunshot. His tragic choice changed the course of many lives, including my own. In addition to my aunt, he left behind three teenage daughters and a five-year-old son, Dan, who came to live with our family while my aunt tried to put together the pieces of her life.

Dan and I became best friends and worst enemies. We did everything together and we fought the whole time. He was the first to learn to ride a two-wheeler without training wheels. I was the first to learn to read. But we were not content with equality; we both wanted superiority.

The battle escalated until the day it reached a peak in our backyard sandbox. Dan and I were arguing, as usual, and my mother was trying to get us to stop, as usual. She warned us that a spanking was her next alternative, but both of us refused to let the other have the last word.

When our arguing reached a decibel level impossible for Mom to ignore, we heard the screen door slam. She marched out to the sandbox, pulled me to my feet, and spanked my rear. I took my punishment without a whimper. Dan got spanked next, but he too refused to shed a tear. Mom repeated the punishment, and we repeated our response.

Our stubborn stoicism frightened Mom. She later admitted that she was afraid we were on our way to becoming hardened juvenile delinquents. After warning us once more to stop fighting, she went back into the house.

Dan and I did stop arguing, but not because of the punishment. We stopped because the argument had become moot; it was no longer possible for either of us to win.

Years later Dan and I told my mother why we both remained stone-faced on that simmering summer day. The subject of our fight had been whether boys or girls were bigger crybabies.

The pride I felt that day for my impressive display of stoicism did not develop into strong character; it grew into disdain for emotion and a stubborn refusal to display any.

Pain is part of every life, and it's human nature to believe that pain is punishment. It's also human nature to try to avoid it. But avoidance can carry a high price tag.

For many years I tried to keep a safe distance from God because I feared that if I made myself noticeable He would punish me for my imperfections. To keep from getting hurt, I would keep my distance. Feeling nothing, I foolishly reasoned, would be better than feeling bad.

Years later I began to question why I could not feel any love for God, a feeling which other Christians seemed to experience and enjoy. The reason, I discovered, was that I had spent so many years trying not to feel anything. I did not yet realize that I could not be whole without being emotional.

> Oh, the comfort, the inexpressible comfort of feeling safe with a person, having neither to weigh thoughts nor measure words, but pouring them all right out, just as they are, chaff and grain together; certain that a faithful hand will take and sift them, keep what is worth keeping, and then with the breath of kindness throw the rest away.
>
> DINAH MARIA MULOCK CRAIK

The suggestion that we should allow ourselves to feel what God feels is frightening, especially to those who have been hurt by someone who claimed to love them. They go to great lengths to avoid feeling anything because the only feeling they know is pain. For some, pain begins so early in

60

life that the only coping mechanism they ever learn is to run from it (often by escaping into bad relationships) or to become numb to it (usually with substances or habits that minimize all feeling).

CHOOSE TO FEEL

A bumper sticker on a blue van caught my attention as I drove downtown for lunch. "Choose to Feel," it read.

Then I noticed the billboards I was passing. Many of them sent a different message, a message urging me to choose things that would keep me from feeling—alcohol to deaden emotional pain; fat-laden food to alleviate feelings of emptiness; luxury cars, diamonds, and other expensive items to lessen feelings of worthlessness. Temptations like these lure us away from God by promising to relieve emotional hurt that is the consequence of sin—our own or someone else's.

God sets a different example. Rather than become numb or indifferent to the pain of sin, God feels all of it. He even allows us to witness Him suffer the results of it. Through the prophet Hosea, God expressed His own heart-wrenching pain caused by the loss of a wayward child (Hosea 11).

When we choose to feel the full range of our emotions—even sadness—we come to a fuller understanding of the God who created us in His image—the image of One who feels.

When we turn off our feelings, or anesthetize them with habits or substances, we rob God of the opportunity to do what He does so well—comfort us; and we rob ourselves of learning how to comfort others:

> [God] comforts us in all our troubles, so that we can comfort those in any trouble with the comfort we ourselves have received from God. For just as the sufferings of Christ flow over into our lives, so also through Christ our comfort overflows.
> (2 Corinthians 1:4–5)

Few people have the patience to listen very long to the erratic beating of a hurting heart. But that's what God wants to do for us, and that's what He wants us to do for others.

In an episode of *Law and Order*, the captain said to Elliot, "Don't worry when you feel something; worry when you don't." I think Jesus would say the same thing.

Shortly after his death in 2003, country music legend Johnny Cash won a Grammy Award for his short video titled "Hurt." The first line of the lyric is "I hurt myself today, to see if I still feel." The remainder of the video vividly illustrates that what makes us feel good one moment can deaden our feelings the next, leaving pain as the only proof that we still can feel.

When we truly want what God wants, we'll begin feeling what God feels. We will weep with those who weep and rejoice with those who rejoice. We'll sorrow over sin and rejoice in righteousness. We'll be angry at every injustice and we'll be eager to dispense grace and forgiveness.

THE OIL OF JOY

Heart disease kills thousands of people every year, and pharmaceutical companies make billions of dollars selling drugs that prevent hardening of the arteries, one of the causes of life-threatening heart disease. In fact, the top-selling drug in the world is one that prevents cholesterol from depositing a plaque-like substance in arteries.

A more serious condition, however, receives little attention and can't be prevented by any wonder drug. It's called hardening of the heart, and the Bible warns against it. "[H]e who hardens his heart falls into trouble" (Proverbs 28:14).

Hardening of the heart ages people more quickly than hardening of the arteries.
FRANKLIN FIELD

A hard heart is one that refuses correction and thus keeps repeating the same mistakes. In the book of Exodus we read about a character who had this condition. The Pharaoh of Egypt refused to release the Hebrew people from slavery when God sent Moses to lead them to the Promised Land. When Pharaoh refused to cooperate, God sent a series of progressively worse plagues to get him to change his mind. But pain to Pharaoh was an annoyance to get rid of, not a warning to heed. As soon as the misery of the plague was removed, he went back to his same stubborn ways.

A COMMON MIDDLE EASTERN fruit is key to the prevention of both hardening of the arteries and hardening of the heart. Several popular diets and many health experts recommend the use of olive oil in place of other fats in our diet. Olive oil is high in good cholesterol and low in the bad kind. It softens arteries instead of hardening them. It's an appropriate symbol for the plea of the psalmist David: "Today, if you hear his voice, do not harden your hearts . . ." (Psalm 95:7–8).

Adding olive oil to our diets won't prevent the spiritual condition known as hardening of the heart. But using it in food can remind us to check the condition of our hearts for symptoms of spiritual hardness such as stubbornness, impatience, bad temper, indifference, and greed.

Today we think of olive oil as something found in decorative bottles and used for cooking. But in biblical times it served so many purposes that it came to be known as a symbol of joy. Olive oil was not only food but also fuel. It was used to anoint kings and heal the sick. It brought pleasure by seasoning food, soothing dryness, creating warmth, and illuminating darkness.

According to today's values, the descendents of Ishmael got the good oil—black gold; whereas the descendents of Isaac got only black olives.

In addition, olives have long been a symbol of peace, which is God's highest desire for His people. Peace with God (shalom) is a world the way it ought to be, a world restored to God's original intention, a world filled with worshipers adoring the One who created them, sustains them, and longs to lavish them with all that is good and pleasing and beautiful.

This is the world we all desire.

FROM EDEN TO GETHSEMANE

From the first to the final garden, the plot of Scripture revolves around desire. In the first garden, desire was perverted; in the last garden it was purified.

Desire determined what Eve did—she wanted food that was pleasing, so she followed bad advice, and evil slithered into creation.

Desire determined what Jesus did—He wanted to please God so He gave up His own life for ours, and innocence returned to creation.

Desire determines what God does—He wants us to know that He loves us, so He does everything He can to convince us that He desires our good by supplying us with beauty and pleasure and love.

Some have a hard time imagining that Jesus, God's perfect Son, could have a desire that was in conflict with His Father, but we know of at least one occasion when He did.

After celebrating the annual Passover dinner with His best friends, Jesus took them to the place they often stayed—an olive garden across the Kidron Valley from the Temple. As they settled down, Jesus asked His friends to stay awake and pray. This was no ordinary prayer request, for this was no ordinary night.

The drama in the olive garden was all about desire—the desires of the Father and the Son were in conflict. Jesus did not want to die. He did not want to bear the weight of the world's sin. He pleaded, "My Father, if it is possible, may this cup be taken from me." But He also wanted to do the will of His Father and to fulfill the purpose for His life on earth. So He added, "Yet not as I will, but as you will" (Matthew 26:39). God, on the other hand, wanted to complete His plan of salvation, and the success or failure of His plan depended on the desires of His Son.

Ultimately, of course, Jesus wanted God's will more than He wanted to save His own life. He wanted to fulfill God's purpose more than He wanted to feel pleasure or avoid pain.

In the beginning, Eve got what she wanted, but not what we needed—the knowledge of evil. In the end, Jesus got not what He wanted, but what we needed—innocence of evil.

Mel Gibson's movie *The Passion of the Christ* presents a gruesome and graphic picture of Christ's final hours on earth. The physical torture is unimaginable, the emotional torment incomprehensible. But for Jesus, the separation and alienation from His Father was far worse than the beatings of the Romans or the betrayal of His friends. Who can imagine being separated from all that is good and beautiful? Who can imagine being in a place where God's grace and mercy don't exist?

The passionate arguments that swirled around Gibson's movie boiled down to this: No one wanted to be blamed for killing Jesus. Even those who don't believe that Jesus is God's Son or Israel's Messiah wanted nothing to do with His death. Some Christians tried to silence the critics by arguing that everyone is equally to blame, but that failed to satisfy those who wanted no part of it.

By allowing the focus to remain on *who was to blame*, people missed the point of why Christ died: He died so that *no one* would have to take the blame.

Jesus came not as the Jews expected—in power and might to rule the earth; He came in weakness and humility to rule in human hearts—precisely the place where the perfect order of creation was first broken.

Christians fail to recognize the ongoing spiritual battle for their hearts, the place where God's glory is reflected.

VINCENTE BACOTE

Jesus came to claim worshipers who delight in Him. He finds them not among people who deny their guilt but among those who believe in the power of His resurrection and gratefully accept forgiveness.

Beauty

IS IT A VICE OR A VIRTUE?

BOTH OF MY GRANDFATHERS were gardeners. They delighted in the beauty of flowers. I never plant flowers or walk through a garden without thinking of them. And I never see daffodils in the spring without thinking of my grandmother.

The last words I heard Grandma say were, "Walking through Daddy's flowers." She repeated this phrase again and again in a slurred, unfamiliar voice as my friend and I, both eleven, tried to get Grandma back into the house after we found her lying in a field of Grandpa's golden daffodils.

My grandfather had died the previous fall, but his flowers, buried all winter in anticipation of spring's glorious resurrection, were unaware that the one who planted them would not be around to welcome them when they poked their heads out of the ground. He was now anticipating an even more glorious resurrection—his own.

Perhaps Grandma was breaking the news to them about Grandpa when she suffered the stroke that would reunite her with Grandpa one week later. Grandma slipped into a coma before slipping off to meet Jesus and Grandpa, and I suspect that the bobbing yellow heads and the sweet scent of Grandpa's flowers made her longing for that better place irresistible.

What is it about a field of daffodils that causes emotions strong enough to carry my grandmother into the presence of her heavenly Father and her loving husband? *Beauty*. What is it about the fragrance of a flower that makes us not want to exhale? *Beauty*. What is it about the taste of a cold sweet beverage on a hot, dry day that makes us savor every sip? *Beauty*. What is it about the sound of a great hymn of faith that brings tears to our eyes? *Beauty*. What is it about the feel of a newborn's soft skin that brings such joy? *Beauty*.

God, in His bountiful love, has created beauty for every one of our senses to enjoy.

Beauty makes us yearn for something more, makes us strive for something better, makes us believe in something perfect. Beauty is God's way of whetting our appetites for all that He wants to give us.

Few people deny the power of

The real sin against life is to abuse and destroy beauty, even one's own—even more one's own, for that has been put in our care and we are responsible for its well-being.

KATHERINE ANNE PORTER

beauty, but some think of it as a vice rather than a virtue, as the lure of God's adversary rather than a gift from God. They see beauty used more often as a vain ambition than a godly goal, as a way to draw attention to self rather than reveal God to others.

Although beauty is a gift from God, it has been corrupted by sin. Having nothing of his own to offer anyone, Satan takes what is good and uses it for evil. He adorns evil with all kinds of glitz and glamor before introducing it to us, and our emotions run away with it before our brain has thought of any questions to ask.

I enjoy reading gardening magazines while soaking in the bathtub, but eventually I become restless. I'm not satisfied to simply view beauty; I want to create my own. So I pull my shriveled body out of the bubbles, get into my gardening clothes, and head outdoors with trowels and pots of perennials.

Going to church should be the spiritual equivalent of reading gardening magazines in the bathtub. Church should be a place where the majesty of God is displayed in such a grand and glorious way that we can hardly wait for the service to end so we can go out into the world and plant a garden of spiritual beauty that will make all who experience it long for a better place.

> Art is the accomplice of love.
> **JANE STANTON HITCHCOCK**

THE POWER OF BEAUTY

Beauty has been the primary factor in convincing me that God is not only great but also good. The beauty of music and the ability God gives us to create it convinces me that God wants us to enjoy life. Singing in choirs has helped me realize that Christianity is more than mental assent to a set of beliefs, and more than agonizing self-discipline to get my body to obey a set of rules. The beauty of music convinces me that living for Jesus involves joy, because God wants nothing but good for all creation, including me.

As I sing, my belief in God becomes more than a mental exercise; it becomes a thing of beauty that stirs passion and a desire for goodness in my soul. Our choir director's ability to pull beautiful music out of mediocre musicians is a metaphor of what God does in my life and in the world. I want to be on God's side not just because He is strong and frightening, but because He is loving and good.

Although truth is certainly important to God, He doesn't expect it to stand alone. God adorns truth with beauty and goodness, making it into something that appeals to every aspect of our being—our hearts and souls and bodies as well as our minds.

TWO THOUSAND WORSHIPERS filled our church on Easter morning, and two hundred choir members filled the loft and lined the aisles for the closing song—a medley of hymns ending with "All Hail the Power of Jesus' Name." As banners bearing the names of God were carried to the front of the church, a spotlight highlighted each one as it moved slowly and majestically forward.

Then came the final banner. As the choir reached the triumphant ending of the song, the banner reached the front of the aisle. In a spontaneous expression of unity, the entire congregation stood in response to the banner bearing the name of Jesus as we triumphantly sang the hymn's final phrase—"And crown Him Lord of all." The choir then began to softly sing "Holy, holy, hallelujah, the Lamb has overcome."

People all around me had red eyes and wet cheeks. My own emotions were so overwhelming that singing couldn't express all that was happening in my heart. The tears collecting in my eyes were like water from a melting glacier. All of the frozen facts about God stored in my head melted that morning. The warm light of Jesus turned my cold, rigid cache of knowledge into a torrent of emotion that poured into my heart and soul. I couldn't imagine why anyone would reject Christ. Nor could I imagine how heaven could be any better than the moment I was experiencing on earth.

The beauty of the music, the passion in our singing, and the choir director's constant admonition to "sing for Jesus" made me want to renounce the sin in my life and take the beauty of Jesus to the world around me.

Much later I realized this experience was an example of how God loves us with all His heart. By placing us in a world filled with beauty and pleasure—all waiting for us to enjoy at no cost—God expresses that He wants what is good for us.

THE POWER OF PRAISE

Around the world, Jewish people still celebrate Passover in much the same way they have for thousands of years. In doing so, they obey God's command to remember His supernatural work of delivering Jacob's descendents from slavery in Egypt. The symbol of their deliverance was the blood of the Passover lamb.

Sincere praise not only pleases God, it also gives us pleasure!

The order of the Passover ceremony builds to a great crescendo and ends in a highly emotional celebration with participants singing and praising God out of sheer delight and enjoyment.

Near the end of the Passover meal, the second half of the Hallel (praise) psalms (Psalms 113–118) are sung. Mark, in recounting the final moments of the last Passover Jesus spent with His disciples, wrote: "When they had sung a hymn, they went out to the Mount of Olives" (Mark 14:26). Imagine Jesus, on the night He was betrayed, on the eve of His crucifixion, singing these words: "This is the day the LORD has made; let us rejoice and be glad in it" (Psalm 118:24). Realizing that these very likely were the last words Jesus sang before His death makes it difficult to sing them to a light-hearted tune.

When the meal ended, the disciples were sleepy from all the food and wine. Eager to find a place to spend the night, they left the city crowded with pilgrims and headed east across the Kidron Valley to a familiar hillside, the Mount of Olives, where they often spent the night.

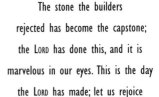

The stone the builders rejected has become the capstone; the LORD has done this, and it is marvelous in our eyes. This is the day the LORD has made; let us rejoice and be glad in it.

PSALM 118:22–24

In the olive garden at the foot of the mountain, the weary disciples, minus Judas the betrayer, settled among the rocks and tried to make themselves comfortable. But for Jesus, the time for comfort had passed.

That night, as the city across the valley finished celebrating the Jewish holy day, Jesus began to feel the weight of the world's sin that He was about to bear. His disciples felt only the weight of their own heavy eyelids, and they were soon asleep.

On that night more than any other, Jesus needed someone to understand His distress, to pray with Him for

God's intervention, to join Him in His suffering. Instead, He began to experience the terror of being alone, totally alone.

In the garden where Jesus prayed, olives were not only grown but also crushed and pressed. The crushing released the oil from the fruit, and the pressing separated the oil from the mashed fruit and pits.

There beside the olive press, Jesus began to feel the crushing weight of the world's sin coming down on Him. And there beside the oil press, He prepared to spill His lifeblood for the world's redemption.

At one time or another, all of us experience the crushing weight of sin. Sometimes it is the weight of our own sin and the shame and embarrassment of having failed miserably. Sometimes we battle temptations that feel irresistible. Sometimes we get trapped in adultery, addiction, or abuse.

At other times it is the load of someone else's sin that weighs us down—someone who betrayed us, deceived us, abandoned us, ridiculed us, cheated us, or made a fool of us. Perhaps it is an unfaithful spouse, a wayward child, or an abusive or alcoholic parent. Sometimes it is another Christian who treats us unjustly.

Think about a time when the weight of that sorrow was so heavy that you couldn't pull yourself out of bed. Now think about the combined grief and pain of everyone in your family, your church, your neighborhood. Add to that all the suffering that sin has caused everyone in your city, state, nation, and the world. Now try to imagine the accumulated grief that sin has caused throughout the centuries since creation. Just for a minute, try to imagine . . .

When God began placing the weight of this sin on Jesus, is it any wonder that the pressure began squeezing the life out of Him? Just as millstones separate the oil from the flesh of the olive by crushing the fruit, the weight of sin crushed Christ and separated His blood from His flesh. Everything true, good, and beautiful lay rejected, deserted, and hideously disfigured in a cold dark cave. Sin put God to the ultimate test.

But Hallelujah! The power of His love overcame the heavy weight of sin. Because of the resurrection we know beyond any doubt that sin—ours or anyone else's—will not and cannot win.

LOVING GOD WITH ALL MY HEART means refusing to let my heart be hardened by the sin and injustice that I have experienced or witnessed. If my heart has already become hard, I pray that the love of Jesus will soften it until it overflows in praise and generosity and kindness and goodness and gratitude. Loving God with all my heart means having every desire satisfied by Jesus. It means having a heart so full of gratitude for God's goodness and beauty and love

77

that it overflows in praise even on the darkest days. When I love God with all my heart, my desires match His. I want what He wants and what He says is good. I feel the way He feels about good and evil.

LOVING GOD WITH ALL MY HEART answers the question "Where did I come from?" *I came from the loving heart of God, and I'm the result of His desire for companionship. Therefore, all my needs and desires can be satisfied only in a relationship with Him.*

REFLECTION QUESTIONS

- ○ What are my strongest desires? How do I satisfy them? Where do I look for satisfaction?
- ○ What do I want that God doesn't want me to have?
- ○ Which of God's commands am I most likely to violate in my attempts to get what I want?
- ○ How do my feelings about God affect my desires?
- ○ In what ways do my actions and attitudes indicate whether or not I believe that God wants to give me what is good?

WITH ALL MY *Soul*

Does It Matter Who I Am?

THROUGHOUT BIBLICAL HISTORY, crossing the Jordan River has represented an act of faith, a spiritual turning point, a new beginning with God.

For me, crossing the Jordan required no faith. I was riding in a bus, so I didn't even have to get my feet wet. It did, nevertheless, represent a turning point. As our bus climbed the barren hillside on the eastern side of the Sea of Galilee, our guide pointed out military bunkers and explained why the land was so desolate. We were entering the infamous Golan Heights, the territory reclaimed by the Israelis in 1967, and the ground was still littered with landmines.

From a lookout point atop the mountain ridge, we gazed down on the farmland along the eastern shore of the Sea of Galilee. Before Israel gained control of the Golan, farmers working at the foot of the mountain used armored tractors to protect themselves from mortar shells fired from above.

Our guide's comments about the present-day Jewish struggle sounded oddly biblical, and I felt as if I had been struck by a Bible released from a time warp. Suddenly it seemed contemporary rather than just historical. God's work in the world did not end when He finished writing His best-selling book. He is still working, still writing people's life stories. But instead of recording them on leather scrolls, He's writing them on hearts and minds as He reclaims souls, one at a time, and restores them for His glory.

During my first trip to Israel I realized that I was not just visiting a place where sacred things happened; I was visiting the people God put in that place to witness those things. Just as many features of the landscape have remained the same for centuries, so have the people. Their looks, their way of thinking, and their passions are much like the people of Jesus' day. Interacting with them gave me a new way of thinking about what it means to be a Christian. I too am a citizen of a special kingdom—a spiritual kingdom. And I should be as passionate about that kingdom as the Israelis are about the nation of Israel.

As we bounced along in the bus, Tony, our guide, gave us a brief history of the Jewish people and then asked: "What does it mean to be God's chosen people?"

From the archives of my memory came an answer. "It means that all the nations of the world will be blessed through you," I blurted.

Immediately I wished I had kept my mouth shut. I didn't want Tony to think I was implying that his people were to blame for the fact that not everyone in the world is blessed.

But Tony liked my answer. "That's exactly right," he said.

The answer was right because it came from Scripture, not from me:

Channels only blessed Master,
But with all your wondrous power
Flowing through us, You can use us
Every day and every hour.

MARY E. MAXWELL

> The LORD said to Abram, "Leave your country, your people and your father's household and go to the land I will show you. I will make you into a great nation and I will bless you; I will make your name great, and you will be a blessing. I will bless those who bless you, and whoever curses you I will curse; and all people on earth will be blessed through you." (Genesis 12:1–3)

The last phrase indicates that all peoples of the earth will receive God's ultimate blessing—salvation—through Israel's Messiah, a descendant of Abraham. But it's also

82

saying that people of faith—people who believe God—are God's ambassadors of blessing to others. We are to be living, breathing examples of our loving, compassionate God. Living in the righteousness of Christ, and in the power of the Holy Spirit, we're to be characterized by justice, fairness, goodness, honesty, truthfulness, purity, and, above all, love.

This Scripture, called the Abrahamic Covenant, is often used to focus on the blessings believers can expect to receive. But God's people are not to become professional consumers of His goodness or giant reservoirs to preserve it. The great crescendo of the passage is not what we're going to get; it's what we have to give. Believers today—just like believers living in the days of Abraham, Isaac, and Moses— are called to be God's channel of blessing to the world.

The Hebrew word translated "soul" in *Shema* (Deuteronomy 6:5) means "breath," which is what God breathed into Adam to change him from an elaborate dustball to a living being (Genesis 2:7).

The Greek word translated "soul" in Mark 12:30 is *psuche,* from which we get the word "psychology." *Psuche* is also the word that is translated "life" in these familiar verses:

> Whoever finds his life will lose it, and whoever loses his life for my sake will find it. (Matthew 10:39)

For whoever wants to save his life will lose it, but whoever loses his life for me will find it. (Matthew 16:25)

A word that gives us a better understanding of this concept is "self." *Psuche* is what makes each of us unique, what sets us apart from everyone else. It's the essence of our identity. So Jesus is saying that we need to give up our "selves."

She tried to be somebody by trying to be like everybody and became a nobody.

UNKNOWN

Women are generally good at this. We seem to have an innate ability to give up our selves. But what we give up ourselves to can cause problems. In adolescence and early adulthood, we give up ourselves to attract boys. To get them to notice us, we devote our time and attention to whatever they spend their time on—even if it's of no interest to us. Advice columnists encourage this by telling young girls to show interest in what boys are interested in. That's the polite thing to do in any relationship. But taken to extremes, it's unhealthy. In college, I spent a whole year "volunteering" in a greenhouse because my boyfriend was doing graduate work at the Tree Research Center. I gained a love for all things green and growing, but I lost valuable time by neglecting my own God-given interests and abilities.

Later in life, women give themselves up to their husbands, children, or careers, depending on which "track" they choose. None of these is a bad choice, but all hold an inherent danger: each can take the place of God in our lives. Anything—even good things—that becomes a substitute for God is an idol.

Idolizing anything or anyone is sin, but the dangerous consequences are multiplied and magnified when we idolize our children. Not only are we neglecting our own souls, but we are endangering their souls as well because we are communicating to them that they are more important than God.

Through counseling, psychologists help patients "find themselves," but the only place to find our true selves is in God. In fact, the only way any of us ever find ourselves is to lose ourselves in God, for that is where we find our true selves—the selves we are meant to be.

The French use the phrase *raison d'être*, which means "reason for being." Loving God with my soul means embracing the truth that my reason for being on earth is to become all that God created me to be—not what my parents dreamed I would become nor what my spouse or children or friends tell me I should be. To do this, I must know God in a way that allows Him to reveal to me my unique abilities and passions. Then I must trust Him to lead me to the place where I can use them to the fullest extent in the way that will bring the most glory to Him.

My life has been blessed by numerous godly influences, so I have a good understanding of the right things to do. After years of practice, I can get myself to do good things. But I often do them for the wrong reasons—to please people, to make myself look good, to elevate myself above others. Instead of losing myself in God, I find myself trying to impress people.

This is the sin that Jesus condemned so harshly in some of the religious leaders of His day. People admired the Pharisees for their knowledge of Scripture and their meticulous keeping of the law. But their motives let off such a stench that Jesus compared them to whitewashed coffins. They did everything outwardly to make themselves look good, but their inner selves were like rotting flesh. They appeared to be the epitome of righteousness, but they were preaching from atop a landfill of their own self-righteousness. Those who had lived their whole lives "in the neighborhood" didn't smell anything

> True love isn't the kind that endures through long years of absence, but the kind that endures through long years of propinquity.
>
> HELEN ROWLAND

foul because it was the only "air" they had ever breathed. But Jesus, having just come from heaven, immediately recognized the stench of spiritual death. The Pharisees weren't loving God with their souls by giving glory to God with every aspect of their being; they were gaining glory for themselves.

In stark contrast to the Pharisees stands the mother of Jesus. Upon learning that she had been chosen to give birth to the Messiah, Mary submitted herself to God with a startling statement that convicts me every time I read it. Her story has become trivialized in countless Christmas pageants, so we have to strain to hear the quiet passion in her response to the angel Gabriel when he visited her one ordinary day and gave her this extraordinary news:

> "You will be with child and give birth to a son, and you are to give him the name Jesus. He will be great and will be called the Son of the Most High. The Lord God will give him the throne of his father David, and he will reign over the house of Jacob forever; his kingdom will never end . . . The Holy Spirit will come upon you, and the power of the Most High will overshadow you. So the holy one to be born will be called the Son of God." (Luke 1:31–35)

Mary didn't run to her mother or girlfriends to get advice about what she should do. She didn't turn to her father or fiancé to ask permission to give an answer. Instead, even though she must have known that disbelief, ridicule, and scorn would follow her all the days of her life, Mary uttered the words that always get stuck in my throat: "I am the Lord's servant. May it be to me as you have said" (Luke 1:38).

By losing herself in God, Mary found her true identity as the mother of God's Son, the world's Savior. And she gave us a priceless gift: a timeless example of what it means to love God with all our souls.

Identity

WHO AM I?

W HEN THE BRIDE-TO-BE asked me to be in her wedding, I was caught off guard because I didn't know her very well. Assuming that she was going to ask me to function in some minor capacity, I managed to say, "Oh, that would be nice."

But then she said, "I'd like you to be a bridesmaid."

My attempt to hide my surprise must have failed because she offered an explanation—one that was even more surprising than the invitation: "I'm asking people who will look good in the wedding pictures," she said.

I was too stunned by her response to consider it a compliment. Besides, I was already calculating the price I was going to have to pay for this unexpected honor. I tried to think of a polite way to decline, but I had not yet learned the art of saying no graciously, so I bought the dress, the shoes, the hair ornament, and I allowed myself to be used as a decoration in her wedding.

Being a bridesmaid was not new to me. I was beginning to wonder if the phrase "Always a bridesmaid, never a bride" was a prophecy concerning my future. Being close to the altar does not count in marriage. In all my experiences as a bridesmaid (twelve), the groom never decided at the last minute to leave with the woman in pastel instead of the one wearing white.

Despite my reluctant participation, the wedding worked for my good. I walked down the aisle with the groomsman who later became my husband. Although the experience cost me more than I could afford at the time, it got me two things money cannot buy: a godly husband and a good illustration.

Each of us has a past that is a scrapbook of things we have and have not been chosen for, and recalling them will likely bring back the same emotions we felt long ago. Maybe you are like me and still can feel the humiliation of standing alone between two teams, the last person to be chosen for a game of softball. When it came to sports, I was always chosen last because my legs are too short for anything that requires speed, and I'm too much of a coward for anything that involves balls flying through the air. Other stories of rejection are more painful to talk about.

Assessments made by others on the basis of how well we

meet their needs are faulty; they have nothing to do with our true worth or our real identity. But they seem right and real, so we believe them, not realizing that they are lies that keep us from hearing the voice of God.

- ○ Fashion voices tell me that I'm a random arrangement of bones (that I must keep strong) and flesh (that I must keep sleek and solid), held together by skin (that I must keep smooth and supple) so that I will be a suitable hanger for the clothes they tell me I should wear. *I am more than a clothes hanger!*

- ○ Government voices tell me that I'm a member of the important middle class (needed to fund projects and programs that keep privileged people in power). *I am not just a taxpayer!*

- ○ Advertising voices tell me that I'm a consumer who urgently needs everything I don't yet have. *I am more than a shopper!*

- ○ Wall Street voices tell me that I'm an investor whose task is to turn a little bit of cash into a lot of profit so that I can enjoy a few pleasures and not become a burden to society before I die. *I am not just taking up space while I wait to die!*

- ○ Technological voices tell me that it doesn't matter who I am or where I'm going as long as I get there first and don't become obsolete on the way. *I am not a machine measured by my speed and efficiency!*

○ Scientific voices tell me that I'm a fluke of nature whose task (ironically) is to improve the human species. *I am not an accident!*

○ Hollywood voices tell me that I'm playing a minor role in a plot so boring that everyone else's "reality" is more interesting than mine. *I am not boring!*

○ Science and Hollywood join voices in an unlikely alliance, shouting these antiphonal reminders: Science shouts that I am here only because my species is the biggest bully, and Hollywood shouts back, saying that I will continue "being here" only if I am able to outwit my neighbors and become the last survivor. *I am not a bully! And I don't have to defeat someone to survive!*

If options like these are the only choices, we may as well concede that evolutionists are right: human existence is just a contest in which the reward goes to the strongest and smartest, sometimes even the cruelest, but certainly not to the kindest or noblest. When life is reduced to competition, the best outcome we can hope for is to hold on for as long as possible and keep ourselves from being pulled apart in a tug-of-war between the competing interests of earth's greedy and power-hungry citizens.

Yet deep within us a voice whispers, telling us that our life is more than the accumulation of random opinions about our usefulness. But what is it?

If sales are any indication of need, a lot of people are still trying to answer the question posed by the subtitle of Rick Warren's bestselling book *The Purpose-Driven Life: What on Earth Am I Here For?* In the first year of publication, the book sold more than ten million copies, breaking the sales record for any book previously published. Although record-breaking sales are good news for the author and publisher, they raise a troubling question for the Christian community: Why are so many of us uncertain as to God's purpose for our lives?

The Bible teaches that each of us is a unique individual designed by a loving God, equipped with certain talents, fueled by particular passions, to fulfill a specific purpose. So why do Christians have such a hard time finding it?

The generation that came of age in the 1970s loved to toss around the phrase "I need to find myself." The phrase often was used as a rationalization for behavior previously considered irresponsible. But somehow it seemed selfish to deny a person the

> Our job . . . is to teach our kids and grandkids to find their identity in themselves as God made them, rather than being swayed by brands and commercialized images—because in allowing themselves to be "branded," they . . . lose their true identity.
>
> CHUCK COLSON

opportunity to "find herself." In fact, it seemed as if the right to such a pursuit ought to be listed in the Declaration of Independence along with the right to life, liberty, and the pursuit of happiness, for how can one find happiness without first finding "self"?

ACCORDING TO THE *New International Encyclopedia of Bible Words*, "Soul is personal existence. It is the life or self of an individual."

Our souls contain the essence of our identity. One dictionary defines soul as "the immaterial essence, animating principle, or actuating cause of an individual life." According to the Bible, the animating force within each human being is the breath of God. We are nothing but a clump of dust until God breathes His life into us. The breath of God in us is our soul, and it is our souls that make us distinct from one another and unique in creation.

> [H]uman beings are more than dust. In the creative act, God not only formed the human body but also "breathed into his [man's] nostrils the breath of life, and man became a living being" (Ge 2:7). Human beings are unique among living creatures, for the life that God created and with which he endowed them is a reflection of his own

image and likeness (Ge 1:26). The body may die, but our individual essence will never be dissolved. (*New International Encyclopedia of Bible Words*)

The word *soul* comes from the Hebrew word *nepes* and the Greek word *psuche*, which both mean "breath." God's breath in us defines our "self." Therefore, any attempt to know ourselves apart from God is doomed to failure.

In the soul . . . lies the individuality—in the case of man, his personality, his self, his ego.
GUSTAV OEHLER

But still we try. In fact, we try all sorts of things— education, careers, possessions, stock portfolios, bank accounts, substances, and relationships.

Early in life we define ourselves by relationships. As children, we are the offspring of our parents. Later we expand the definition of self to what we do. While we're in school we are students. Then we go on to become accountants, administrators, artists, doctors, editors, engineers, farmers, musicians, nurses, politicians, teachers, scientists, social workers, writers, or a myriad of other occupations. Some of us become wives, and we change our names to identify ourselves with our husbands. Some of us also become mothers, and we become known as "Mom." But even in the best of situations, these titles are temporary. All of them can be taken from us; none provides a permanent identity. And when we're stripped of titles and tasks, and sometimes even relationships, we're no longer sure who we are.

Whenever we go through a period of transition, it's common to experience a crisis of identity. After focusing on one task for a long time, we feel lost when it's finished. If we identify ourselves by what we do, the feeling of being unnecessary is tantamount to having no identity. This is especially true if what we do is connected to what we are called and who we are related to.

Being a mom carries with it both a name and a job description. So it's no wonder that someone who has been called "Mom" for many years starts to question who she is when she no longer hears the urgent call of a toddler yelling "Mommy," or the demanding whine of a teenager pleading, "Mom!"

> You can take away everything I do, but you can't take away who I am.
>
> JIM EMERY

Due to a series of unrelated circumstances one year, I lost my place in my family, my business, and my church. During that time I had to answer some difficult questions: Which part of my identity transcends the titles I hold and the tasks I perform? Who am I when I'm separated from people I love, places that are familiar, and positions that give me meaning and significance?

Some of us keep our fragile selves propped up by avoiding situations where loss, failure, or rejection is likely. But in doing so we risk missing God's plan for our lives. One of those places may be precisely where God wants to display His glory in us.

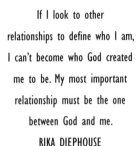

If I look to other relationships to define who I am, I can't become who God created me to be. My most important relationship must be the one between God and me.

RIKA DIEPHOUSE

Deity

AFTER A FAILED ATTEMPT at delivering his fellow Hebrews from Egyptian slavery, Moses dashed off to the desert and hid for forty years. When God showed up and told Moses to go back and try again—this time in God's power and timing—Moses was less than enthusiastic. In an attempt to disqualify himself from the assignment, Moses raised the question of his identity. "Who am I to lead these people?" He demanded of God. This response was somewhat disingenuous in that forty years earlier Moses was already thinking of himself as Israel's deliverer (Exodus 2), but God graciously ignored that detail.

God could have given His frightened friend a pep talk about how well equipped he was for the task, but He didn't. He could have recited Moses' life story, reminding him of how he had been spared from death at infancy, reared in the king's palace, and prepared in the sheep fields of Midian to learn—by practicing on sheep—the difficult task of leading difficult people. But there was no "You can do it if you try" talk from God. God was more concerned about having Moses know who God was than in bolstering Moses' self-confidence.

Instead of answering the question Moses asked, God told Moses what He wanted him to know: In essence He said, "Moses, you're asking the wrong question. Before you can find out who you are, you need to find out who I am."

Moses needed confidence in God, not in himself, and for that reason he needed *not* to be reminded of who he was but of who God was. And that is where all questions of identity need to begin.

IF YOU WANT TO HAVE SOME FUN, start a theological discussion and try to get someone to ask, "Who is God?" Then say, "I am."

When the person sarcastically responds, "And who told you that you are God?" say, "I didn't say 'You are God,' I said, 'I am.'"

If you're clever enough, you might be able to prolong the dialog and become famous for creating a theological version of Abbot and Costello's classic comedy sketch about baseball: "Who's on First?"

Or you could quote Exodus 3 and explain that "I am" is the name God gave Himself when Moses wanted to know what to call Him.

For a long time, I wondered why God would call Himself by such an odd name, but here's what I've come to understand. One of the first lessons of grammar is that a sentence needs only two things to be complete: a subject and a verb. So when God says His name is "I am," He is saying that He is complete. He is the subject, and He is the action. He is matter, and He is motion. He is everything there is, which is everything we could possibly need.

God expanded on the meaning of His name throughout His encounters with humans. In fact, in a series of brief interactions with Moses, God led him through three stages of revelation. First, God said His name was "I am." Then God added two words, saying, "I am the LORD." Finally, by adding two more words, God made one of the most stunning pronouncements of history. He said, "I am the LORD *your* God." The creator of the universe made Himself personal. He affirmed to Moses what He had told Abraham:

> "I will establish my covenant as an everlasting covenant between me and you and your descendants after you for the generations to come, to be your God and the God of your descendants after you." (Genesis 17:7)

In addition to making Himself personal, God set Himself apart from all other gods by choosing to reveal Himself. The Bible is not a "how-to" or "self-help" book; it's an autobiography. God is telling His life story so that we can know Him, and in knowing Him, know ourselves as He knows us. (See 1 Corinthians 13:12.) We are all characters in God's autobiography, and our lives are pages in the unfolding drama of redemption.

The Bible says that God created us in His image, so a flawed image of God will keep us from knowing ourselves. If

It is true that all people are created in the image of God, but Christians are supposed to be conscious of that fact, and being conscious of it should recognize the importance of living artistically, aesthetically, and creatively, as creative creatures of the Creator. If we have been created in the image of an Artist, then we should look for expressions of artistry, and be sensitive to beauty, responsive to what has been created for our appreciation.

EDITH SCHAEFFER

we have created a mental image of God out of the dust of our own experiences, we have constructed a false God.

Experience alone leads to wrong conclusions about God. Bad experiences lead us to think that God is mean, uncaring, and impossible to please, or that we are simply unlovable. Good experiences lead to the false conclusion that God just wants us to be happy no matter what we do or how we live, or that we are just getting the good that we deserve. All such self-conceived ideas about God need to be tested by Scripture.

The prophet Isaiah painted one of the most simple yet beautiful word pictures of God found in the Bible: He who "measured the waters in the hollow of his hand" and "with the breadth of his hand marked off the heavens," "comes with power" yet "tends his flock like a shepherd" (40:10–12). Isaiah depicted God as being both strong and gentle, both above us and with us.

But even creation with its vast oceans and majestic mountains, and all of Scripture with its histories, poems, and prophecies, could not adequately represent God. He had one final word to say about Himself, and that word is Jesus.

Divinity

WHO IS JESUS?

JESUS LEFT THE COMFORT AND SAFETY of heaven to put flesh on God's bare-boned answer to Moses' question "Who are you?" God said of Him: "This is my Son, whom I love; with him I am well pleased" (Matthew 3:17). Among the details that Jesus added to explain His Father's name, and to expand on what it means to bear the name "I am," are these:

- ○ *I am* the Alpha and Omega, the First and the Last.
- ○ *I am* the way, the truth, and the life.
- ○ *I am* the bread of life.
- ○ *I am* the light of the world.
- ○ *I am* the good shepherd.
- ○ *I am* the resurrection and the life.
   (from Revelation 22:13; John 14:6; 6:48; 8:12; 10:11; 11:25)

God added to the testimony of His Son, revealing even

more about His identity, in the writings of the apostles. To believers living in Colosse, Paul expanded on Christ's list of "I ams" with this amazing "He is" list:

- ○ *He is* the image of the invisible God, the firstborn over all creation. (Colossians 1:15)
- ○ *He is* before all things, and in him all things hold together. (1:17)
- ○ *He is* the head of the body, the church. (1:18)
- ○ *He is* the beginning and the firstborn from among the dead, so that in everything he might have the supremacy. (1:18)

The whole concept of God taking human shape had never made much sense to me. That was because, I realized one wonderful day, it was so simple. For people with bodies, important things like love have to be embodied. That's all. God had to be embodied, or else people with bodies would never in a trillion years understand about love.
JANE VONNEGUT YARMOLINSKY

Then, in a stunning statement that is nearly lost because it is one of several in the passage, Paul wrote:

God has chosen to make known among the Gentiles the glorious riches of this mystery, which is *Christ in you*, the hope of glory. (1:27, italics added)

After hearing everything that Paul said about Christ, the Colossian believers came to the surprising words "Christ in you."

104

People living in that part of Asia believed in gods that were impetuous and impersonal, who hovered above the people, lived in man-made temples, and demanded mutilating self-sacrifices from their followers. The notion of a God who would come down, make a personal sacrifice, and take up residence in His followers . . . well, no one had ever heard of such a thing.

Later in the letter, Paul added another unheard-of idea: "For *in Christ* all the fullness of the Deity lives in bodily form, and *you have been given fullness in Christ*, who is the head over every power and authority" (2:9–10, italics added). Not only was Christ in them; they also were *in Christ*.

The mountain journey is about becoming more aligned with God's presence and purposes in our lives. . . . The goal is not the glamour of iridescent light, but Christ-shaped encounters with others. The journey is not about getting out of this world or out of ourselves into some more glamorous place—but about getting as deeply into this world as God, in Christ, has.
ROBERT C. MORRIS

One of the mistakes we make in trying to determine God's purpose for our lives is that we reduce it to decisions related to what we should *do*, such as where we should go to school, where we should live, whom we should marry, what career we should pursue, and what job we should take. Then we compound our faulty thinking by falsely assuming that right choices will lead to fairy-tale endings.

105

While "what to do" decisions are important, the Bible indicates that they are secondary. The first question each of us must ask about ourselves is "Am I in Christ?" Regarding this, Jesus made two important statements: speaking of Himself, He said, "the Son can do nothing by himself; he can do only what he sees his Father doing, because whatever the Father does the Son also does" (John 5:19). And of His followers, He said, "apart from me you can do nothing" (John 15:5).

Before we can *do* anything, we must be *in* Christ.

Community

WHERE CAN I FIND MYSELF?

"YOU ARE SUCH A LOSER!" These words are meant to hurt, and they do. The old response "sticks and stones may break my bones but names will never hurt me" is little comfort. It fails to acknowledge that not all injuries are physical. Words *do* hurt, and some of the most serious hurts are those that damage our souls—and name-calling is an assault on a person's soul. God designed us to be truthful, so our "default setting" is to believe what we hear. When we are called a disparaging name, we tend to believe it. It hurts to be called a loser because it says that we are worthless. But it's a lie.

Even though I am no longer a child, I still feel bad when someone refers to me in an unfavorable way that makes me feel like a loser. Now, however, whether the accusation comes in actual words or a subtle attitude, I have a new way of thinking about it. I know that from God's perspective, losing can be gaining. So in my mind, I say to the person, "Thank you so much for the compliment. That's the best thing you could say about me. Jesus said I couldn't find my life without losing it, so I am losing my old self to find a better self in Jesus. I'm losing my anger, bitterness, and hatred, and I'm finding God's mercy, forgiveness, and love."

When we lose ourselves in Christ we can begin finding our true identity. "[W]hoever wants to save his life will lose it," Jesus said, "but whoever loses his life for me will find it" (Matthew 16:25). The Greek word translated "life" in this verse and "soul" in the great commandment (Mark 12:30) means "self." When we lose our "selves" for Christ, we find out who we are meant to be.

> When people say, "I need to find myself," I think if they really search and find themselves, they may be quite disappointed. It's in finding God that we know ourselves.
>
> PHIL KEAGGY

As we begin to find our true selves in Christ, however, we make a troubling discovery about our identity. We learn that we are not God, that the world does not revolve around us, and that we must relinquish the right to rule because we are filled with all kinds of nasty thoughts and desires that are not at all godlike.

The first identity crisis each of us faces is finding out that we are not the center of the universe. This is a hard truth to accept after the blissful days of early childhood when everyone around us behaved as if we were the most important creature on the face of the earth. The transition can be long and difficult, with many setbacks. Once we are removed from center stage, we have many choices to make, and the truth is, we make many bad choices. These send us scurrying back to the center where we try again and again to take up residence and to reorder the world to revolve around us. Knowing, however, that it's not where we belong, we pretend that it's not where we want to be. Yet we still think, subconsciously at least, that it's the only safe place to be.

Being bumped off center stage is traumatic, but it's only the beginning. Finding out who and what we are *not* clears the stage for us to discover *who we really are.* The early scenes are reason for despair, and many stomp off stage in anger. But those who pay attention to what the Playwright is saying, and who persevere to the end, are compensated beyond measure.

Humility is facing the truth. It is useful to remind myself that the word itself comes from humus, earth, and in the end simply means that I allow myself to be earthed in the truth that lets God be God, and myself his creature. If I hold on to this it helps prevent me from putting myself at the center, and instead allows me to put God and other people at the center.
ESTHER DE WAAL

ACT ONE: I Am a Wretch

Some people don't like the hymn "Amazing Grace" because they don't like singing the phrase, "that saved a wretch like me." Frankly, I don't see what the big deal is. God referred to Jacob, whom He loved, as a worm (Isaiah 41:14). And the good news of the gospel is that even wretches and worms can be loved by God and redeemed for a noble purpose. (See Romans 5:8.)

With God, being honest about who we are leads to a relationship, not rejection. Jesus proved this in His encounter with a woman of not-so-noble character. Tired from a long journey, Jesus sat down beside a well in a town that most self-respecting Jews would go the extra mile to avoid. Then He started a conversation with a woman no self-respecting Jew would speak to. Notice how He turned a daily chore into a spiritual lesson.

When Jesus asked the woman for a drink, she expressed surprise that He would speak to her (John 4:7–9). Jesus indicated that He wasn't who she thought He was, and she expressed interest in knowing who He was (vv. 10–12). Instead of identifying Himself, however, Jesus told her what He had to offer: water that would satisfy her thirst (vv. 13–14).

In a surprising reversal, the woman then asked Jesus for a drink (v. 15). When Jesus asked her to go get her husband, she explained that she didn't have one.

Instead of attacking her for what He knew was an evasive answer, Jesus commended her for telling the truth. Then He told her something about herself that she wasn't eager to have known: that she'd had five husbands and was living with a man to whom she was not married (v. 18).

The woman then recognized that Jesus was a prophet (not because of what He said about Himself but because of what He knew about her, v. 19) and steered the uncomfortable discussion away from herself by bringing up the impersonal subject of where to worship (v. 20).

Jesus changed the subject back to something personal—from "where" to worship to "who" to worship (vv. 21–24). The woman, trying again to make it impersonal, expressed faith that the Messiah would one day explain everything (v. 25).

Seizing the opportunity the woman opened up by mentioning the Messiah, Jesus told her who He was with a simple "I am" statement: "I am he," He said (v. 26).

Note how Jesus kept the conversation going. He didn't tell the woman how bad she was. He just kept increasing her thirst (like salt) for more knowledge about Himself. He didn't condemn her for who she was or what she was doing wrong. He gently led her to discover who He was and what He could do for her.

When the disciples rejoined Jesus, the woman returned

to her village. Later in the passage we learn that many in the town believed in Jesus because of the woman's testimony (v. 39). However, it wasn't what Jesus said about Himself that convinced them; it was the truth He spoke about the woman. She returned to her neighbors urging them, "Come, see a man who told me everything I ever did," (v. 29). After meeting Jesus, she was no longer ashamed of who she was. She had met someone who knew her intimately but whose foremost desire was to redeem her, not condemn her.

Seeing ourselves as we are is the first step toward becoming all that God designed us to be.

One reason I believe the Bible is true is because it doesn't whitewash the leading characters. Even the best of them are revealed to have flaws. Unlike humans, God does not cover up the faults of His favorite people. How foolish, then, for me to think that He will help me hide mine. After all, Moses warned the Israelites that their sin would surely find them out (Numbers 32:23). This passage is often used as a scare tactic to keep people from sinning, and maybe it has some effect. But still we sin, so perhaps it should also be used to encourage confession. After all, being the first to admit our own sin is better for our souls than waiting to be accused of it by someone else. The New Testament gives further support to this idea: "Therefore confess your sins to each other and pray for each other so that you may be healed" (James 5:16).

Scripture on this subject is troubling because it says that we should reveal what we want to conceal (our sin) and conceal what we want to reveal (our good deeds). In His most famous sermon, Jesus said, "Be careful not to do your 'acts of righteousness' before men, to be seen by them. If you do, you will have no reward from your Father in heaven" (Matthew 6:1).

Honest confession about who we are keeps the cause of Christ moving forward. Denial, cover-up, and secrecy sap the energy of Christian communities and keep people focused on the past.

With God, confession is the first step to a relationship, not to rejection. Imagine if it were the same with us. Imagine if we learned to interact with sinners the way Jesus did. He had a way of making people understand that His concern was not to call attention to their sin to condemn them for living badly, but to redeem them for a better way of life.

ACT TWO: I AM GOD'S CHILD

When I answered the late-night phone call, I had no idea what lay ahead. My father was in the emergency room after falling and injuring his eye. The next morning I met Mom and Dad at the eye surgeon's office.

When the doctor started to take the bandage off Dad's eye, Mom said, "You probably don't want to look, Julie."

I agreed, and stood just outside the door, thinking I was a safe distance.

It seemed, however, that everyone in the office wanted to see what I did not want to look at. Some crowded into the small examining room. Others stood outside the door near me. Like I said, I thought I was safe. But even though I could not see my dad's injured eye, I could see the horror in the eyes of those who did. One kind nurse—trying to comfort me I'm sure—put her hand on my shoulder and said—over and over—"Poor Dad, poor Dad, poor Dad."

Sometimes too much kindness can make a person weak. The more pity I received, the weaker I became. The weakness hit my stomach first, and I felt powerless to hold down all the coffee I'd been drinking. Just in time, the feeling of "losing it" moved from my stomach to my head and then to my eyes. When the lights started going out, I quickly found a chair and sat down. Immediately, a comforting blanket of darkness covered me, and I felt relieved to no longer see or feel anything.

But all too soon one of the nurses invaded my protective covering. "Are you okay?" she asked. "Can I get you something?"

"Some water might help," I said.

She brought me a cup of ice water, and by the time the doctor had once again covered Dad's eye, I was feeling well enough to listen to the bad news.

Somehow in the fall Dad had not only ripped off the cornea transplant he'd received several years earlier, he'd also managed to mangle the retina. The doctor offered little hope that my father would regain sight in that eye, but said he couldn't be certain until after surgery.

Outside the room, my mom started to cry. "I just want things to be the way they were yesterday," she said.

"I know, Mom," I said. "But nothing's going to be the same for a few weeks."

She cheered up a little at the idea that this was only a temporary setback, and then we wheeled Dad over to the surgical wing of the medical center.

Later I thought about the many emotions that overloaded my circuits that day. I thought about all of those strangers looking inside my father's head, and I realized, metaphorically, that I knew very little about what went on in there. I'd always been told that I was a lot like my father, but I knew very little about him. I wondered if my reluctance to get to know him better was due to the fear that I would find out more about myself than I wanted to know. Then I considered my reluctance to get to know God, and I realized that it too has to do with trying to avoid the truth about myself.

As I thought about the fall that had left Dad sightless in one eye, I thought about The Fall (capital "F") that has left all of us spiritually sightless. And then I thought about a heavenly Father who wants nothing more than to have His children look into His eyes and see who He is so that we can stop hiding who we are.

IN A REGENT COLLEGE CHAPEL SERVICE, Professor Paul Stevens said, "God has called you into relationship with Himself . . . before we are called to do something, we are called to some One. . . . We won't find out who we are without finding out Whose we are. Never forget Whose you are, because that is who you are."

In his later years, the apostle John wrote these words about who we are:

> How great is the love the Father has lavished on us, that we should be called children of God! And that is what we are! (1 John 3:1)

What better news to hear than finding out that we are the beloved children of the Maker and Sustainer of all creation?

ACT THREE: I AM A WITNESS

Identity theft is on the rise, say those who claim to know. But how can identity be stolen? I realize that my social security number, my credit card numbers, and my bank account numbers can be taken and used fraudulently. But these numbers do not add up to my identity. I am more than a collection of numbers connecting me to my earthly "riches," and anyone who implies otherwise is committing another kind of identity theft by reducing me to the sum of my bank balance.

Another form of identity theft is more serious, and it's one that we perpetrate against ourselves. It's a form of spiritual suicide that we commit when we try to be someone other than who we are. To become like someone else who is already beautiful or popular or talented or intelligent seems easier than discovering our own gifts and abilities, passions and desires, and finding a place to use them.

As a writer, I struggle with this. Whenever I sit down in front of my computer, I wish I could make my words sound like those of Henri Nouwen or Anne Lamott or Philip Yancey. They don't. If anything, my words sound more like those of an impatient preacher. I want to be soothing, not scathing; amusing, not accusing; inspiring, not indicting. Sometimes I wonder if the prophet Jeremiah wanted to write like David, the singer and songwriter, or like Moses, the historian. Or was he content to speak in the style and for the purpose that God assigned him, even though his message was unpopular?

"We are called *into* God's kingdom and glory" (1 Thessalonians 2:11–12) "*by* His own glory and goodness" (2 Peter 1:3–4) "*for* the praise of his glory" (Ephesians 1:12) "*to* share in God's glory" (2 Thessalonians 2:13–14, italics added).

We cannot be an effective witness for God if we insist on using someone else's voice or talent or experience. Being a witness is more than memorizing the plan of salvation so that I can explain it to strangers; it is telling others the truth about myself and my personal encounter with God. It means being able to say "I once was," but now "I am." In the words of the hymn writer, "I once was lost, but now am found, was blind, but now I see."

One summer I worked at a Christian camp, and one of our duties was to go to a nearby resort town and do street evangelism. The idea of stopping total strangers on the street and "witnessing" to them about God seemed phony to me. To be a witness a person has to have seen or experienced something. The Bible is clear about that. One of the Ten Commandments is "do not bear false witness." Standing on those lakeside streets, I felt like a false witness even though I was a Christian. I believed God. I trusted Christ. I did not deny my sinfulness and was grateful to accept forgiveness.

But I did not have the kind of dramatic conversion experience that I thought was needed to make a convincing case for God.

I became a Christian at age eight—before sin had a chance to reach the fullness of its ugly potential in my life; the "was but am" aspect of my testimony was not at all compelling.

Since then I have learned that my testimony doesn't have to be dramatic. My witness is the simple story of my life. It's my first-hand account of how God is taking the "me" that He created and is gently and lovingly transforming and restoring it to its full potential for His glory. Slowly but surely He is turning me from a clump of clay to a work of art.

The Greek word translated "workmanship" in Ephesians 2:10 is *poiema*, from which we get the English word *poem*. This means that we are God's poem, His artistic expression. We are God's good work!

I still feel some residual guilt from those early failed witnessing attempts. But I am somewhat consoled when I remember that Moses didn't start his public ministry until he was eighty years old, and even Jesus didn't start until He was thirty. Looking back, I believe that I was being required to do something I was not equipped to do. I was being sent to "go, tell" before doing the prerequisite "come, follow." I had not yet seen what God had done, was doing, and could do in my life. I didn't realize that I had not simply been saved *from* the consequences of sin but also saved *for* the cause of righteousness.

While writing this book, I received an e-mail requesting that I write a short description of myself for an author biography. The request asked that I leave out "the marital status/family stuff and the academic degrees." They wanted me to "keep it light and fun." Since Jesus described Himself metaphorically, I tried doing the same:

> I am a magnet for factual debris. Like Pigpen in the *Peanuts* comic strip, who lives under a cloud of dust, I live under a cloud of disconnected fragments of stories, observations, experiences, and information. My role in the universe, like a crime scene investigator, is to figure out how these seemingly unrelated fragments fit together to reveal truth; then I form them into a shape that will help me (and hopefully others) see that truth more clearly.

The way I am made in the image of God is that I take dust (in my case, words and information) and mold it into something useful (i.e., knowledge and wisdom). I don't need a big budget, a big staff, or a big audience to accomplish this. I only need eyes that can see God, ears that can hear Him, and a heart that is willing to look for God in every experience and to reveal God in every encounter. (I also need the patience to let God decide if, when, how, and where to use my service.)

Poet T. S. Eliot wrote:

> *Where is the Life we have lost in living?*
> *Where is the wisdom we have lost in knowledge?*
> *Where is the knowledge we have lost in information?*
> *The cycles of Heaven in twenty centuries*
> *Bring us farther from God and nearer to the Dust.*
>   *(from "The Rock")*

My assignment is to reverse the process Eliot wrote about. I am to arrange the particles of dust that come to me in a way that points people to God. But that is all I can do. The rest is up to God.

My life motto, based on 1 Thessalonians 1:5, is "Anyone can put words on a page, but only God can breathe life into them." Unless God breathes life into "the work of my hands,"

Jesus, fill now with your Spirit
Hearts that full surrender know
That the streams of living water:
From our inner selves may flow!
MARY E. MAXWELL

which I pray that He will do, everything I write will be a lifeless idol.

ACT FOUR: I Am a Worshiper

One week before Jesus was crucified, a woman named Mary poured a whole bottle of expensive perfume on His head and feet. Then she did something even more remarkable: She wiped His feet with her hair.

Not only did Mary sacrifice what may have been her life's savings in this extravagant act of worship, she also sacrificed her reputation. Respectable women in that culture never even let down their hair in public, much less do anything as audacious as Mary did. To worship Jesus, Mary was willing to be considered immodest, perhaps even immoral. She knew that true worship was letting down her hair and making herself vulnerable. Today, many of us think of worship as putting our hair up and making ourselves unapproachable.

Some people attend big churches because they can hide there. They feel safer when they remain unknown. But this contradicts the purpose of being part of a church. A church needs to be a place where it is safe to be known—a place where we can reveal our weaknesses and find strength, not where we have to conceal our faults to appear strong.

Worship is the one task for which we all are chosen. Life

on earth is our great rehearsal, and Jesus is our great worship leader. In the prelude to the greatest worship service the world has yet experienced, Jesus ate the Passover meal with His friends. Writing about that evening, the apostle John said, "Having loved his own who were in the world, he now showed them the full extent of his love" (John 13:1). This is John's account of that evening:

> When [Jesus] had finished washing their feet, he put on his clothes and returned to his place. "Do you understand what I have done for you?" he asked them. "You call me 'Teacher' and 'Lord,' and rightly so, for that is what I am. Now that I, your Lord and Teacher, have washed your feet, you also should wash one another's feet. I have set you an example that you should do as I have done for you. I tell you the truth, no servant is greater than his master, nor is a messenger greater than the one who sent him. Now that you know these things, you will be blessed if you do them. (John 13:12–17)

The disciples still did not know how radically different their lives were going to be before the night ended, but this was certainly an indication. The world they lived in was being overturned in much the same way that Jesus, earlier that week, had overturned the tables of those who were corrupting worship in the Temple. Jesus was redeeming worship, and He was about to do it by making Himself the sacrifice. Like witnessing, worship has to be personal, and it has to be done willingly. True worship is an act of love. It's giving up our "selves" in service for God and others.

> The greatest, most beautiful expression of our creativity is to find a way to give ourselves.
>
> MICHAEL CARD

GRAND FINALE: I AM A BRIDE

As the sun set behind us, a line of weary hikers moved slowly up a rocky Turkish hillside toward the ruins of a church built to honor the martyred apostle Philip. Upon reaching the site, we gathered inside the octagonal structure to take Communion—to remember the death of Jesus in the place where one of His first followers had been savagely executed.

Our teacher, Ray VanderLaan, spoke of the new covenant Jesus announced to His disciples the night before He died. Linking the customs of the Passover cup and the Jewish marriage cup, he explained that Jesus, in saying to His disciples "This cup is a new covenant in my blood," as He offered them the cup of salvation, was, in essence, telling the disciples that He wanted them to be His bride. In taking the cup, the disciples accepted His proposal.

While meditating on the amazing concept of the church being the bride of Christ, I recalled another Turkish location, Antioch, where followers of Jesus were first called Christians, or "Christ ones." Like a bride, Christ's followers were called by His name.

As I took the cup, I had a hard time swallowing the juice. I thought of the places I had been—the other worship settings I had seen. Those who worshiped pagan gods came to their ceremonies dressed in white but went away covered in bloody stains from their own self-mutilating sacrifices. In contrast, my God used His own blood to wash away my stains and present me pure and spotless, like a bride dressed in white, adorned for her husband. I was overwhelmed with gratitude that Jesus wanted me as His bride and would take the risk of letting me be called by His name.

I think about how careful I am about how my own name is used. I think about the projects I choose to work on—and the ones I don't because I would be embarrassed to have my name attached to them. I think about the people I associate with; I choose people I can trust not to hurt me.

Then I think about all the unlikely people God has chosen to be called by His name. Suddenly the distinction between humans and God is unmistakable. Like grooms choosing brides, and brides choosing bridesmaids, and captains choosing players, we humans tend to choose people who make us look good. But God chooses people He can make good.

God chooses those who are judged "losers" by the world's standards and makes them the beneficiaries of His riches. He chooses the lost and leads them home. He chooses those who are unclean and unkempt and does such a thorough clean-up that they become a bride adorned for His Son:

> Christ loved the church and gave himself up
> for her to make her holy, cleansing her by the
> washing with water through the word, and to
> present her to himself as a radiant church, without
> stain or wrinkle or any other blemish, but holy
> and blameless. (Ephesians 5:25–27)

In his vision on the island of Patmos, the apostle John saw four living creatures seated around God's throne who kept repeating the same few words. "Day and night they never stop saying: 'Holy, holy, holy is the Lord God Almighty, who was, and is, and is to come'" (Revelation 4:8).

I used to think, *What a boring existence!*

But I no longer think that. Instead I think about what it's

like spending time with someone I love, or doing something I love to do. I don't want to leave; I don't want to stop. I want time to stand still.

That must be what it's like for the special creatures in John's Revelation. I try to imagine the scenes they have witnessed from their position around God's throne. I consider how amazed they must be at God's patient and loving involvement with wayward earthlings. And then I think, *What other response could there be? What else is there to say but "Holy, holy, holy"?*

Is it boring to say the same words over and over? Not when I'm in the presence of the One I love. Not when I'm doing exactly what I was designed to do.

Like all creation, each of us is designed to glorify God. So life will be an amazing adventure if we remain in Christ and live and love in the power of His Spirit for the glory of the Father. For God created us, knows us, loves us, and has a special purpose for us.

Praise to the Lord!
O let all that is in me adore him!
All that hath life and breath,
come now with praises before him!
Let the amen sound from his people
again; gladly forever adore him.

JOACHIM NEANDER

LOVING GOD WITH ALL MY SOUL means rejoicing in every breath I take, because the air that gives pleasure to my lungs and life to my whole body reminds me that every moment is a gift from a living and loving God who created me in His likeness, who called me to bless the world on His behalf, and who allows me to bear the name of His perfect Son.

LOVING GOD WITH ALL MY SOUL answers the question "Who am I?" *I am a one-of-a-kind person made in God's image with unique talents and abilities, passions and motives, opportunities and experiences, that are best used in a community of believers to glorify God and further His kingdom.*

REFLECTION QUESTIONS

- ○ What talents and abilities do I have?
- ○ What passions motivate me?
- ○ What mix of qualities and abilities makes me unique?
- ○ Am I listening to God telling me who I am or to others telling me who I should be?

WITH ALL MY *Mind*

Does It Matter What I Think?

WHY CAN'T EVERYONE JUST GET ALONG? We all say we want peace, so why is there so much conflict?

The simple answer is: We can't get along because we can't agree on such basic things as right and wrong, good and bad, just and unjust.

If these conflicts were just between unbelievers we could understand. But Christians battle one another as well. And since we all claim to worship the same God—*the one true God*—our disagreements raise the question of whether we are really worshiping God or our individual ideas and perceptions of Him.

Even though we are blessed to have sixty-six books of Scripture and centuries of Christian history to teach us, we have many of the same disputes as the early church.

Little has been written as to why Jesus added "mind" to

the Greatest Commandment (Mark 12:30), but the apostle Paul gave a clue in his first letter to the church in Corinth.

Much of the New Testament was addressed to a Gentile audience, primarily those influenced by the Greeks. In contrast to the Jews who were looking for signs, the Greeks were looking for wisdom (1 Corinthians 1:20–25). To them, *mind* was the center of life.

As the seeds of the gospel were sown outside the land of Israel, some began growing in thorny places where paganism, with its many gods and goddesses, had long been the prevailing belief. In the city of Colosse, located in what is now modern day Turkey, new Christians were stumbling over their pagan roots. They wanted to add Jesus to their list of deities rather than honor Him as the one true God. They wanted to keep their religious practices which gave "the appearance of wisdom with . . . their harsh treatment of the body" (Colossians 2:23). (We do much the same thing. Workaholism, for example, is harsh treatment of the body that gives the "appearance" of wisdom.) Paul responded to such heresies with these words: "Set your minds on things above, not on earthly things" (3:2).

WHAT IS MORE SOOTHING after a trouble-filled day than stepping outside on a star-studded evening and gazing heavenward? Who can peer into the night sky and not forget, at least for a moment, the cares of life on earth? Ancient Israel's prolific songwriter wrote a poem thousands of years ago that still rings true:

> When I consider your heavens,
>   the work of your fingers,
> the moon and the stars,
>   which you have set in place,
> what is man that you are mindful of him,
>   the son of man that you care for him?
>   (Psalm 8:3–4)

When we try to imagine the immensity of God's heavens, our problems do indeed seem trivial. Yet God doesn't think so! With all of the galaxies He has to attend to, God is mindful of us! And not only are we on His mind—He cares for us.

No wonder the apostle Paul advised young believers to set their minds on things above. For in doing so, we raise our thoughts above the level of earthly disputes and focus instead on a loving heavenly Father who wants us to know Him, to know how to live peacefully with one another, and to know that we can live eternally with Him in a place even more beautiful than this planet.

To best enjoy our brief time on earth and to prepare for

life in heaven, we must bring our thoughts into agreement with God. As we do, we learn all the good that God has in mind for us, and we begin to love Him with all our minds.

In a letter written about the same time to another church, Paul pleaded with two women living in Philippi "to agree with each other in the Lord." He urged others in the congregation to help them, and in this case he actually told the people what to think:

> The mind controlled by the
> Spirit is life and peace.
> ROMANS 8:6

> Finally, brothers [and sisters], whatever is true, whatever is noble, whatever is right, whatever is pure, whatever is lovely, whatever is admirable—if anything is excellent or praiseworthy—think about such things. (Philippians 4:8)

Imagine how blissful life would be if everyone thought only about things that are excellent and praiseworthy! The temptation, of course, is to imagine a world in which everyone agrees with our own definitions of these words. But the "formula" only works when everyone agrees with God's definition:

> [D]o not let yourselves be conformed to the standards of this world. Instead, keep letting

yourselves be transformed by the renewing of
your minds; so that you will know what God
wants and will agree that what he wants is good,
satisfying and able to succeed. (Romans 12:2 The
Complete Jewish Bible)

Imagine! Created beings not only can *know* the mind of
the Creator, we can *know* that what He wants for us is good,
satisfying, and able to succeed.

Agreeing

THAT GOD IS RIGHT

ONE NEAR-DEATH EXPERIENCE made me change my driving habits forever.

It started with an ordinary bike ride. I hopped on my ten-speed and headed down a busy two-lane street with a 55-mph speed limit. Partway to my destination, I hit a stone in the road, lost control of my bike, and went hurtling headlong across the pavement. Just then a car went whizzing past. If the driver had been passing me as most drivers do—without moving into the passing lane—I would have been road-kill. But he went around me as if passing a car—and by doing so he spared my life.

As I said, the experience changed the way I drive. I now pass bicycle riders as I would pass a car—by pulling over into the left-hand lane. It also made me passionate about changing the way others drive—particularly my husband.

Jay has been improving. On our way to visit friends recently, he waited until it was safe and then steered the car into the left lane to pass a person riding a bike. "Did you notice how I passed that kid?" he asked. "I did it because I know it makes you happy."

As soon as the words were out of his mouth, I realized that my strategy to protect bike riders had failed. If Jay does it only to please me, he probably does it only when I'm in the car. I want more than that. I want him to agree that my way of passing people on bikes is the best way to drive, not just my own paranoid personal preference.

The ways of the LORD are right; the righteous walk in them, but the rebellious stumble in them.

HOSEA 14:9

For years I believed that the highest motive for doing good was the desire to please God. But when Jay's desire to please me left me unsatisfied, I began to doubt whether my own feeble desire to please God was satisfying to Him.

Yes, God wants me to obey because I want to please Him. But He also wants me to obey because I agree with Him about what is right and good. He wants my mind as well as my heart to be aligned with His.

People often say that the three words they long to hear are "I love you." Running a close second must be the words "You are right." I know parents who long to hear those words from their children, which makes me think that God longs to hear those same words from us.

The word *righteous* has been relegated to the dusty dictionaries of theologians. But being righteous is our way of saying to God, "You are right."

The whole assembly responded with a loud voice: "You are right! We must do as you say."
EZRA 10:12

The English word *righteous* is derived from the Old English words *right* and *wise*, and it means to act "in accord with divine or moral law; [to be] free from guilt or sin" (Merriam-Webster).

No offense, Merriam, but to act in accord with *moral* law will not make anyone free from guilt or sin. It will only make us *self*-righteous, which is the condition that Jesus so vehemently opposed. It might also be the unforgivable sin, because those who are *self*-righteous have no reason to think they need the righteousness of Christ.

The word *righteous* in the New Testament is the English translation of the Greek word *dikaios*, which refers to "the person whose way of thinking, feeling, and acting is wholly conformed to the will of God."

Before any of us can be truly righteous, we must acknowledge that it is God's right, not ours, to determine what is right. Our part is to learn what God says is right and then to submit our minds to His transforming work until we agree with Him.

AGREE ABOUT WHAT IS GOOD

I often use phrases like "That looks good . . . sounds good . . . smells good . . . tastes good . . . or feels good." According to my definition, "good" is whatever pleases me.

God is not opposed to pleasure. In fact, His first formal worship setting made provision for the enjoyment of all five of our senses. We call the first house of worship a tabernacle, but it was really a tent—a very elaborate tent! It housed an ornate, gold-covered ark that held the stone tablets God gave to Moses on Mt. Sinai. (God is not against beauty.) It had an altar of incense where priests were to burn a blend of fragrant spices made by a perfumer. (God approves of pleasant aromas.) It had an elaborate table with plates and pitchers. (God appreciates a well-appointed dining experience.) Around the tabernacle were curtains made from colorful yarn and finely twisted linen. (God appreciates color and texture.) Skilled musicians were appointed to lead worship. (God enjoys pleasing sounds.)

God values what looks, sounds, smells, tastes, and feels good, and He wants us to enjoy these things. But He does *not* want us to worship them; He wants them to remind us to worship Him, the creator and giver of all good things, and

He wants our enjoyment of them to be an act of worship. If we think of our senses as being purely for pleasure, we'll eventually think that whatever brings us pleasure is good, and that's bad!

Consider this partial list of what the Bible says is good:

○ It is good to be near God (Psalm 73:28).

○ It is good to praise the Lord and make music to His name (Psalm 92:1).

○ It is good to make requests, prayers, intercession, and thanksgiving for everyone—including kings and all those in authority—that we may live peaceful and quiet lives in all godliness and holiness (1 Timothy 2:1–4).

○ It is good for our hearts to be strengthened by grace, not by ceremonial foods (or other rituals) (Hebrews 13:9).

Goodness is *not* what pleases us; it's what pleases God. When our minds are aligned with God, we'll choose things that please Him, which eventually will bring pleasure to us as well.

A YOUNG WOMAN FROM MY CHURCH believes that "It is good to praise the LORD" (Psalm 92:1), and she is determined to do so despite how she feels. Jill and her husband, Darren, suffered more tragedy in four years than most of us will experience in a lifetime. Three of their children, all in infancy, died of a rare genetic disorder. Less than a year after the death of their third baby, Jill was diagnosed with breast cancer, requiring aggressive treatment. Yet the darker her circumstances became, the brighter her witness shone. Through everything, she was a testimony of God's faithfulness, even when He was leading her through the valley of the shadow of death. In Jill's words:

> The Lord has given to us and He has taken from us and through it we have to choose to continue to praise Him. It's certainly not easy to stand in front of your child's coffin and say, "Yes, Lord, I praise you." It's not; it's impossible. But that's where He comes in. He doesn't leave you alone to suffer. He offers to walk beside—to give hope to the hopeless and peace where there is no peace to be found. He alone gives us the ability to praise Him when He asks us to walk through the longest desert.
>
> The first day that I got chemo I sat in the chair looking at that tube going into my port, unbelieving that this body was really mine, unbelieving that I was receiving chemotherapy. Then the song "Blessed Be Your Name" by Matt and Beth Redman came on my player. The

questions and the grief came in waves as the medicine flowed in. How could I continue to praise Him? How long would we be required to walk the road marked with suffering? How, Lord? How? How long could we go on like this? How long, Lord? I listened over and over.

Throughout these last couple years I've doubted. I've questioned. I've wondered at His plan and thought for sure that mine was better. But when it comes down to it I know it's a choice. A choice to praise Him even when life seems like it's just one terrible thing after another, a choice to praise Him when things are going so well that it seems like we don't even need Him. It's a choice—a choice with eternal consequences. A choice that is life-changing—not only for yourself but also for those around you.

Jill chose to follow the pattern established by ancient Israel's most famous songwriter. Even the darkest of David's songs contains praise, not because his circumstances were great but because he knew God was good.

AGREE ABOUT WHAT IS SATISFYING

Early in my editorial career I worked on a book by

Gary Smalley titled *Joy that Lasts*. The book was based on the metaphor of a cup, and Gary's premise was that dissatisfaction came from "filling his cup" with all the wrong things, though not necessarily bad things. When he stopped expecting to find fulfillment from people, places, positions, and possessions, and started looking to God instead, he found the elusive satisfaction.

To be satisfied, many think we need a spouse, children, love, understanding, acceptance, health, money, success, respect, approval, sex, vindication, more time, a better job, and perhaps even revenge. But the Bible has this to say about satisfaction:

- If we delight in the Lord, He will satisfy our desires (Psalm 37:4).
- God's unfailing love is satisfying (Psalm 90:14).
- God satisfies every living thing (Psalm 145:16).
- God invites all who are thirsty and poor to come to Him and He will satisfy them with all that is good (Isaiah 55:1–2).
- If we spend ourselves on behalf of the hungry and satisfy the needs of the oppressed . . . the Lord will guide us and satisfy our needs even in dry places (Isaiah 58:9–11).

Being a Christian involves more than accepting the claims of Christ because we like the idea of having Him pay for our sins so we can be spared the consequences. Christianity is a way of life that invites God to transform our thinking until we realize that everything He wants for us is good.

The cup metaphor helped me understand that obedience is not engaging in a futile struggle to empty my life of all that's bad; it's gladly filling my life with everything that God says is good. God doesn't want to drain pleasure out of life; He wants to fill life with purpose and meaning that enhance pleasure.

After the apostle Paul told the people living in Colosse to set their minds on things above, not on earthly things (Colossians 3:2), he seemed to do the exact opposite by bringing to mind a whole list of earthly things that they were to rid themselves of (v. 8). However, the very next paragraph suggests that the way to rid ourselves of earthly things is to fill our minds with heavenly thoughts—compassion, kindness, humility, gentleness, patience (v. 12), forgiveness (v. 13), love (v. 14), peace and gratitude (v. 15). The "secret" to doing this is tucked in the center of the paragraph: "Let the word of Christ dwell in you richly as you teach and admonish one another with all wisdom, and as you sing psalms, hymns and spiritual songs with gratitude in your hearts to God" (v. 16).

Simply put, when the singing and teaching of God's

Word is flowing into our lives, all fears and doubts and evil thoughts and desires are washed away in the current.

AGREE ABOUT WHAT IS SUCCESSFUL

My idea of success is to receive positive recognition for something I've done. But here again, God's idea is different. Scripture has this to say about success:

- ○ Anything done in disobedience to God cannot succeed (Numbers 14:41).
- ○ Success comes only after obedience (Joshua 1:6–9).
- ○ David had success because God was with him (1 Samuel 18:13–16).
- ○ Nothing succeeds against the Lord (Proverbs 21:30).
- ○ All "earthly" success is temporary and doomed to failure once God's plans have been accomplished (Daniel 11:36).

Even though words are "my business," I have not always used them well, or even honestly. The place where I first recall using words dishonestly was, sadly, in an Old Testament Bible Survey class. During each class period the professor would pass around a clipboard with every student's name on it. At the top of the page was one question: *Did you read the assignment?* We had to place a check mark beside our name in one of two columns: "yes" or "no."

If we checked "yes," we got an A for the day. If we checked "no," we failed.

To read the entire Old Testament in one semester was no simple task. I didn't want to settle for anything less than an A, however, so I made sure I read every word. To make the assignment manageable, I made up my own definition of the word *read*. I decided that it meant "to focus my eyes on a word." So that's what I did. I consciously looked at every word in every verse of the assigned reading.

Using my definition, I could speed through the assignment while completing other tasks—eating, filing my nails, chatting with roommates. And best of all, I could keep my conscience clear when I checked "yes," I had "read" the assignment.

But a clear conscience is not proof of right behavior (1 Corinthians 4:4). When making the assignment, the professor had more in mind than merely looking at words. He intended that I would convert the words from information into knowledge as they moved from my eyeballs to my mind.

God's goal for the reading of His Word is even more lofty. When the words of Scripture settle into our brains as knowledge, He desires that we recognize the knowledge as truth; that the truth will then flow from head to heart and be converted into love; and that love will then seep into every area of our lives, eventually finding its way into other lives as we go about living and breathing the beauty and truth of God's Word.

"He defended the cause of the poor and needy, and so all went well. Is that not what it means to know me?" declares the LORD.

JEREMIAH 22:16

In my misguided attempt to keep up my grade point average, I was failing in something much more important: truthfulness. I also was missing the opportunity to become something much better than a good student; I was failing to become a godly person.

People today operate with much the same mindset that guided me as a college freshman: we define truth in a way that enables us to succeed in whatever goal we have set. Some even argue that telling partial truths isn't bad as long as we do it for a good reason (e.g., to get something done cheaper, faster, or with fewer hassles). But anything attained dishonestly does not fit God's definition of the word *success*. True success comes only when we agree with God about how to achieve it.

WHAT GOD HAS DONE

THE CHURCH I ATTEND does not follow the liturgical calendar, but I participate in Lent, the forty-day-period preceding Easter when Christians remember Christ's sacrifice for us by making a sacrifice of our own.

To avoid having frequent reminders of my failure, I generally give up something that isn't a big temptation for me. This small sacrifice does not make me more spiritual, but it does make me think differently. Fasting does not prove my goodness; it convinces me of God's, for it reminds me that God is the provider of all good things. Even my failure to fast successfully isn't bad because it reminds me that no one is good except God alone (Mark 10:18).

Throughout Scripture God emphasizes the importance of remembering, and He encourages the use of memory devices. One of the first examples is in the first book of the

Bible, where we learn that God placed a rainbow in the sky to remind Himself of His promise to never again destroy all life with a flood (Genesis 9:13–16).

Many years later, when Moses addressed thousands of recently freed slaves and their families, he told the people to use memory devices to help them remember God's commandments:

> Tie them as symbols on your hands and bind them on your foreheads. Write them on the doorframes of your houses and on your gates. (Deuteronomy 6:8–9)

God told the Israelites to remember such things as the Sabbath (Exodus 20:8); the things they had seen (i.e., what God has done, Deuteronomy 4:9); that God had brought them out of slavery (Deuteronomy 5:15); the Lord, His laws, His decrees (Deuteronomy 8:11); that God is God and there is no other (Isaiah 46:9).

To help His people remember, God established an assortment of holiday celebrations during which they were to stop working and take time to remember and enjoy everything God had done for them (see Leviticus 23).

Christians have a set of holidays that also serve as memory devices; they help us to remember the life and work of Christ.

Scripture itself is another memory device. The stories of the Bible remind us of God's work in the past to redeem creation. Our own stories, or testimonies, remind us of the work God is doing today.

Several years ago my mom completed a project that I had been pestering her to do for years: she finished writing part one of her life story.

Over the years Mom had come up with many reasons for not doing this. Her best excuse was her fear that remembering would bring back too many painful memories. This was difficult for me to refute because it would be wildly selfish of me to say, "Do it anyway because I want to know my family history."

Eventually I encouraged her to think of it another way. "After all these years, do you think you might have a different perspective on some of the things that happened?" I asked. "Maybe writing about them will actually make them *less* painful." The thoughtful look on her face encouraged me to continue. "Getting them out of your mind and onto paper might even be therapeutic."

Shortly after that she started writing, and little by little her story took shape. When it was finished, we chose pictures to include and had it printed and bound. We then gave copies to family members at a special reunion. My mom's story included the account of how my grandparents had come to faith in Christ after their daughter, my mom's older sister, died of tuberculosis at age 19. I sometimes wonder how different my life would have been if the aunt I never knew had not died at an early age, for her death was a turning point in Mom's family.

> Dad always felt that Ruth's death was the Lord's way of bringing him to God. What a tragic thing to have happen to get a person to come to Christ, and I think this was very heavy on Dad's heart for many years. I do believe the Lord uses this means, not as a punishment, but when he can't get us to respond to his call in any other way. How much simpler and better it would be for people to realize their need for salvation through Christ without such saddening circumstances.
>
> Our lives changed much after this happened. Dad had always been very rough talking with nearly every sentence interspersed with swear words. After this he very seldom used any bad language and never used the Lord's name in vain. I asked Aunt Frankie a short time before she died if she remembered the change in Dad. She said the entire family noticed it and talked about it because they didn't think such a change could

ever happen to him. But it was really a blessing to us. (Arlene Ackerman)

Writing our life stories and telling others about our spiritual journeys is a way to remember and proclaim God's faithfulness: "I will sing of the LORD's great love forever; with my mouth I will make your faithfulness known through all generations" (Psalm 89:1).

Although each child must come to personal faith in Christ, it's important for believing parents and grandparents to communicate the story of their own spiritual pilgrimage (see Deuteronomy 6).

Through the way we live and the stories we tell, we create memories for the next generation. Will they remember how we defended ourselves and our way of life or how we defended the poor and needy? Will they remember our attitudes of hate and vindictiveness or our words of love and compassion? Will they remember the stories we tell about the unfaithfulness of humans or the faithfulness of God? Will they wonder why we believe or know why we do?

Thanks to my parents and grandparents, my spiritual heritage provided fertile soil for my own faith to grow.

 Knowing

WHO GOD IS

LIVING OUT OF A SUITCASE requires a skill that I lack:
organization. So whenever I travel, I put my limited abilities
into high gear. On a trip a few years ago, my best efforts
failed.

After getting out of the shower on our last morning in
the hotel, I couldn't find my clean underwear. I searched
for several minutes before asking my husband if he had seen
them.

"Were they in a plastic bag?" Jay asked.

"Yes," I answered.

"Well, there were two plastic bags with clothes in them,"
he announced, as if the information would be news to me.

"I know," I said, "So where are they now?"

"I combined them."

"Why would you do that?" I moaned.

"I was just trying to help you get organized."

"But I *was* organized. The white bag was for clean and the brown one was for dirty."

"I'm sorry. I didn't know," he apologized. "They all looked the same."

"Where are they now?" I asked.

"I put them all together with my dirty clothes."

After going through a week's worth of dirty laundry I found some underwear that seemed clean. When I finished getting dressed, Jay sensed that it was safe to speak again, and he said, "I don't want this story turning up in 'Our Daily Bread.'" (One of the drawbacks of living with a writer is that you do sometimes find stories about yourself showing up in print.)

The thought hadn't occurred to me until he mentioned it, but a possible application came quickly to mind. The book of Leviticus says, "You must distinguish between the holy and the common, between the unclean and the clean" (10:10).

In a world still swirling in sin thousands of years after its catastrophic collision with evil, the need for discernment is critical, and God has assigned to His followers the task of knowing the difference between good and evil. What separates God's people from everyone else is the wisdom He gives that enables them to discern holy from common, sacred from profane, clean from unclean, good from evil.

I thought that was the end of the lesson I was to learn from dirty underwear, but shortly after we got back to Michigan another incident provided yet another insight. One afternoon I had to be gone for several hours. When I got home, I discovered that Maggie, our dog, had "buried" some of my dirty underwear under Jay's pillow. I must admit that I had a hard time wiping the smile off my face.

Maggie has learned to discern clean from unclean. Unfortunately, she prefers unclean. Old smelly clothes are as comforting to her as some of my old dirty sins are to me.

The kind of discernment that God wants His children to learn, of course, requires more than physical senses; it requires a relationship with the One who created us and who knows what is good for us, so that we not only know what is good but also understand why it is good for us to choose it.

SOME PEOPLE WANT to leave to experts the study of God and His relationship to the world, but this doesn't seem to be God's plan—at least not for our generation. Jesus said, "From everyone who has been given much, much will be demanded; and from the one who has been entrusted with much, much more will be asked" (Luke 12:48). We often think of "much" as referring to financial resources and material possessions, and so we give cash to churches and charities. But that's not what Jesus was talking about. He was talking about *knowledge*—in this case, the servant's knowledge of the master's will. If we know what's expected of us and don't do it, we're more guilty than those who are ignorant.

Who knows more about God's expectations than our generation? Who has been given more knowledge, more revelation (Creation, Christ, and the complete text of Scripture), and more teaching than people alive today? Who has more copies of Scripture, more Bible study tools, more opportunities to learn about God than people living today in the United States?

God is revealing Himself to everyone, not just a few. This means that theology is for all of us, not just "the professionals," for what we believe about God affects our marriages, our families, our work, and everything we're involved in. The writings of the prophet Jeremiah indicate why it's so important for everyone, not just professional clergy, to know God.

The religious experts in Jeremiah's day were misrepresenting God by prophesying "the delusions of their own minds" (Jeremiah 23:26). They were leading people astray with "their reckless lies" (v. 32). Due to their dishonesty, the people did not know the true nature of God—that He "exercises kindness, justice and righteousness on the earth" (9:24).

Some people today, although they call themselves

Christians, are showing the world a picture of an angry, vengeful God who is looking for any reason to annihilate them rather than a kind and compassionate God who is earnestly trying to convince them to believe His Son and accept His forgiveness.

Knowledge is important, but it's not enough. Discernment is important, but it's not enough. We also need to know how to use knowledge and discernment as God intends—not to harm people and make enemies for God but to help people and make friends for Him.

LEARNING ABOUT GOD FROM CREATION

While on vacation, Jay and I went to see the mountains of the Pacific Northwest. We arrived at Mt. Rainier late in the afternoon and hurried into the park. On the way up the mountain we stopped at various lookouts and took pictures of what we thought was Mt. Rainier.

Upon reaching Paradise Lodge, however, I realized that I had been taking pictures of the wrong mountain. It was beautiful, but it wasn't the one we had come to see. Mt. Rainier was shrouded in clouds. I had to ask people to tell me where the mountain was. Then I had to trust that what they told me was true. I pointed my camera into the clouds and snapped a few pictures so I would have some evidence that I had been there.

The next day was even worse—heavier clouds and rain. I decided I'd better stop fussing about what I could not see and start enjoying what I could! After all, I was surrounded by one of my favorite color combinations—green and white. The soft greens of emerging deciduous trees highlighted the darker shades of the forest evergreens. Fog formed by evaporating snowfields hovered above the trees and swirled between them like ghosts reluctant to leave. In many places, the taller trees pierced the fragile fog with their pointed tops. Waterfalls created by melting glaciers cut jagged white lines from the undulating clouds to the forest floor. Green poked out from the remaining snow. At lower elevations some wildflowers bloomed. I was witnessing the awakening of the forest. So what if the mountain wanted to hide?!

I didn't need to view the majesty of a mountain to witness the amazing work of God. His wonder is equally evident in tiny plants that can survive harsh, brutal winters because God properly equips them. If rock formations rising out of the earth reveal God's strength and grandeur, the emerging new life of plants and animals reveals His tenderness.

That was the message I needed to receive from God, and I accepted it with gratitude. Even if I didn't see the top of the mountain, I had seen enough to remind me that creation is a stunning work of revelation and a jubilant call to worship.

On our third day at the foot of Mt. Rainier, we awoke to a hazy blue sky. *Could it be?* We hurriedly packed our suitcases, ate our breakfast, loaded the car, and still the sun was out. But was the mountain? We drove into the park one more time.

At every turn of the winding road we looked up through the trees, up to the top of every glacier-filled crevasse. Not far into the park, I saw my first glimpse of Mt. Rainier's glory. Jagged lines of black granite rose in brilliant contrast to the white snow and blue sky.

Higher than any of the huge peaks around it—7,500 feet higher than the mountain I previously thought was "it"—Mt. Rainier was indeed the reigning king of mountain peaks. There was no uncertainty once I saw it. I felt foolish for having been deceived by such a short imposter. Rainier was high and dangerous, but bright and beautiful.

As we stood at its foot and gazed at its face, I thought of the passage in John's gospel about Jesus and the Samaritan woman. As a result of the woman's testimony about her encounter with Jesus, many believed. But wanting to know more, they urged Jesus to stay, which He did. Later they said to the woman, "We no longer believe just because of what you said; now we have heard for ourselves" (adapted from John 4:4–42).

Previously I believed people's testimony about the

mountain, but now my personal experience made the truth real. I knew for sure that the witnesses who had seen it had been telling the truth.

In e-mails to friends back home, I had joked that if we never saw Mt. Rainier from below the clouds, maybe we could see it from above them when we flew home. With that thought in mind, I boarded the plane with my camera hanging around my neck.

As the plane rose toward the west and then circled to the east, I spotted the mountain rising above the cloud cover. I raised my camera and started taking pictures past the young woman in the window seat. She politely moved forward and backward so I could get the best angle, but she showed no interest in looking out the window.

"You must live around here," I said. "I take it that you've seen the mountain before."

"I can see it from my bedroom window," she said. "I've grown up with it."

I thanked her for letting me take pictures and then got settled for the three-hour flight. I took my Bible from my carry-on case to catch up on some reading I had missed while searching for mountains.

"Do you study theology?" the young woman asked me.

"Not formally," I said, "but I'm a Christian, and I believe the Bible tells me what I need to know about God and the meaning of life and how to live, so I try to follow it, even though I fail a lot."

"I'm trying to find a religion," she said. "My father is Buddhist, so I'm interested in that, but my mother is Episcopalian. She just gave me a Bible, but it's so big I don't know where to start reading."

I showed her the book of John in the New Testament and explained that the four gospels all tell the story of Jesus' life, but that John is probably the best one to read first to get a basic understanding of Christianity.

She asked more questions, and I explained, as briefly and simply as I could, what makes Christianity different from other religions. I told her about Jesus, about His death and resurrection, and how we can have our sins forgiven because of what He did on our behalf.

Later, as I thought about our discussion, I wondered, Was my explanation of Christianity like a boring discourse on the history of a mountain or like an artist's rendition of its beauty? Did I convey to her that Christianity is even more beautiful than Mt. Rainier and even more important to pursue? Did I communicate the beauty of my faith or just facts? Did I describe my faith as being not just true but also strong and magnificent? Did the picture I showed her make her curious enough to want to see more? Did my "postcard" explanation describe Jesus in a way that made her eager to see and experience Him for herself? Will she now seek to find the one true God with as much enthusiasm as I sought a vision of the real Mt. Rainier?

I thought of the similarity between the two of us. Her familiarity with Mt. Rainier was like mine with Christianity. Having grown up with it in my background, I often take Christianity for granted, not realizing that many have never seen a clear view of it and are still looking into the clouds, hoping to see the real thing, yet often being deceived by inferior imposters.

Before we got off the plane, I handed the young woman a business card and invited her to contact me if she had any questions. Whenever I think of her, I pray that God will protect the few seeds I was able to sow, that He will enable them to survive the brutal climate of today's popular culture, and that they will grow into a thriving plant.

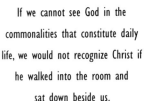

If we cannot see God in the commonalities that constitute daily life, we would not recognize Christ if he walked into the room and sat down beside us.
DON C. SKINNER

God has His reasons for not letting me see certain things. In the case of Mt. Rainier, He wanted me to see something more important than a mountain's grandeur. He wanted me to see His lavish, reliable tenderness so that it would be fresh on my mind when He placed me next to a young woman who needed to hear about God's loving kindness and compassion for all who seek Him.

Creation holds innumerable lessons about God like this one. We just need eyes that can see.

Learning about God from Scripture

After observing some all-too-public disagreements between Christian leaders, I joked with some friends that someone ought to write a book titled *If God Is Such a Great Parent Why Can't His Children Get Along?*

A short time later I was listening to an interview with one of my favorite authors, Philip Yancey, when I heard Philip say, "I probably shouldn't say this on radio, but, if I had to summarize the story of the Old Testament, I would use this phrase: It was God learning how to be a parent."

Was that true? I wondered. Did God have to *learn* to be a parent?

As I thought about this, I realized that yes, the Old Testament does show a vibrant picture of an amazing God who, though He Himself remains changeless, willingly changes His methodology. But does He change methods because He's "learning" to be a parent? Could it be instead that God changes strategies so He can reach as many people as possible? Long before the apostle Paul used the phrase, "I have become all things to all men so that by all possible means I might save some" (1 Corinthians 9:22), God has been doing exactly that.

I wouldn't argue about this because the way God tells the story it does indeed sound as if He's learning. But perhaps God portrays Himself this way because He's trying to communicate on a level we can understand. God didn't wait until He sent Jesus to start lowering Himself. He's been doing it all along. After creating the earth, God didn't vacate the premises. He stayed around to socialize with His creatures. Apparently He enjoyed spending time with them.

As far as we know, Adam and Eve are the only two humans who didn't start life as children. Scripture indicates that God created them, shall we say, post-puberty. And from what we read in Genesis, God walked with the young couple as their friend, not as their creator, their ruler, or even as their Father.

But all that changed when Adam and Eve traded truth for a lie. As soon as they tried to tip the balance of power in their favor, they fell right off the scale.

Since then God has been working to restore the relationship between Himself and His creation. As part of His strategy He seems to be sending the human race back to the part Adam and Eve skipped—childhood.

So instead of saying that the Old Testament is the story of God learning to be a parent, I would say that it's the story of humans learning to be children. Jesus said, "I tell you the truth, unless you change and become like little children, you will never enter the kingdom of heaven" (Matthew 18:3).

One of the most important things children learn as part of a family is how to get along. Jesus' cousin John said, "This is how we know who the children of God are and who the children of the devil are: Anyone who does not do what is right is not a child of God; nor is anyone who does not love his brother" (1 John 3:10). And, "If anyone says, 'I love God,' yet hates his brother, he is a liar. For anyone who does not love his brother, whom he has seen, cannot love God, whom he has not seen" (1 John 4:20).

So back to the original question: "If God is such a great parent, why can't His children get along?" It's because we're all behaving like children trying to prove that *we are right*, and that "Daddy loves *me* best." It's the spiritual equivalent of sibling rivalry, and it has no place among Christians.

The central message of Scripture is summarized in these words of Jesus: "A new command I give you: Love one another. As I have loved you, so you must love one another. By this all men will know that you are my disciples, if you love one another" (John 13:34–35).

LEARNING ABOUT GOD FROM JESUS

After a leisurely dinner at one of our favorite restaurants, a walk to the lighthouse at the end of the pier in Grand Haven, Michigan, followed by coffee at a local coffee shop, my husband and I and a friend headed home. Feeling relaxed from the exercise, invigorated by the conversation, and buzzed from the caffeine, I began telling a story.

When I was young, our family often went to the shoreline of Lake Michigan for picnics during the warm summer months. On the way to the beach stood a home that we called "the messy house." Every time we passed it, both coming and going, someone would yell, "Drive slow, Dad, so we can see the messy house."

Every time we drove past, we could see the ironing board set up in the middle of the living room, and it was always heaped with piles of stuff. Clutter also covered the furniture.

The messy house was one of the wonders of my young life. What seems odd to me now, however, is not how messy it was but how visible it was. Whatever time of the day or night we drove past, the drapes were wide open, and in the evening the lights were on. Not only did the family live in chaos; they didn't even try to hide it.

The story ended there, but I didn't have the sense to stop talking. "I still like it when people leave their drapes open and the lights on so I can see inside their houses," I added, my nose pressed against the car window as we drove through a residential area.

"What do you like about it?" our friend asked.

"I like knowing that other people are as messy as I am."

"And why is that?" he probed.

"It makes me feel better about myself."

"Why does that make you feel better?"

"Because at least I keep the drapes pulled so no one can see my mess," I blurted.

As soon as the words were out of my mouth, I knew that I had unintentionally jerked open the draperies that hid my own messy life.

I stopped talking then, but it was too late. Without a moment's hesitation our friend flicked a switch that flooded the scene with light.

"I guess that means you like seeing other people's messy lives but you're not willing to let them see yours," he said.

For a moment the light blinded me, but soon I saw what I had tried to hide: Vulnerability is something I recommend for others but reject for myself.

Ironically, I was once complimented for making myself vulnerable in my writing. I thanked the person, but I was thinking, This isn't true vulnerability. I'm not really making myself vulnerable. I'm simply trying to make myself acceptable by giving my character flaws a pleasing personality and making them entertaining. My self-disclosure has more to do with exhibitionism than true vulnerability.

Self-exposure, of course, is the beginning of confession, but confession that stops at exposure has nothing to do with virtue. If it did, all the people who tell their perverted stories to talk-show hosts would be candidates for sainthood. Today's talk shows are a counterfeit confessional. People seem to think that by exposing their perversions they'll find acceptance, but what they really need is redemption.

Confessing sin to gain acceptance for it falls far short of the idea expressed in James 5:16: "Therefore confess your sins to each other and pray for each other so that you may be healed." True confession does not cause people to chuckle at sin; it causes them to weep. And the motive behind true confession is not a desire for admiration; it's a longing to be healed.

When we stop trying to make ourselves look good to others we have the opportunity to learn about true vulnerability. Vulnerability is *not* whitewashing our lives with religious activities and self-imposed rules which allow us to rationalize that we have no need for accountability. Vulnerability is acknowledging to ourselves and admitting to others our areas of weakness so that they can watch for signs of waywardness and gently nudge us back on track before we plunge into the abyss of serious sin with devastating consequences.

God exhibited the highest form of vulnerability when He

dressed His Son in the thin skin of humanity and made Him the most vulnerable of all people: an infant. Christ was the embodiment of vulnerability because He was "susceptible to being wounded or hurt; open to criticism or temptation; open to attack or assault."

When I get the courage to try being vulnerable, I look for someone who loves me and will not use my secrets to hurt me. But God made Himself vulnerable to those who hated Him, who ridiculed His goodness, rejected His love, and eventually killed Him.

The baby in the manger did not come to win a popularity contest; He came to win our redemption by allowing Himself to be hurt so that we could be healed. He didn't come to gain acceptance for Himself before the world; He came to gain acceptance for us before God.

Believing

WHAT GOD SAYS

"JUST BELIEVE" IS A POPULAR SLOGAN that decorates everything from sweatshirts to wall hangings to Christmas cards and ornaments. But the kind of faith this slogan advocates has more to do with the mystical power of positive thinking than anything God ever said on the subject. It gives the idea that faith is nothing more than a spiritualized form of wishful thinking.

Although it's silly to talk back to a slogan, I want to ask, "Believe what?" Believe that God will repay money we foolishly borrow? Believe that God will neutralize the consequences of our bad choices? Believe that God will give us the car, career, or spouse of our dreams if we promise to behave in a certain way? Believe that God will make a sugar-laden dessert nourishing if we pray before we eat it?

Faith is not convincing ourselves that we have God's

stamp of approval on our plans; faith is believing that God's plans are better than ours.

That's what Noah believed. So, at God's instruction, he set about building a houseboat to save himself, his family, and a remnant of the animal kingdom from the flood God said was coming, even though Noah had no idea what was coming because he'd never in his life seen rain.

That's what Abraham believed. So, at God's command, he left the comfort and familiarity of home and headed across the desert for a place God said was better, even though Abraham had never seen it.

That's what Moses believed. So, by faith, he refused the privileges rightfully his as the son of Egypt's ruler and identified himself instead with people God said He had chosen for Himself, even though they were still slaves belonging to Pharaoh.

Biblical faith is not about taking foolish chances; it's about taking on the identity of Jesus. It's not about having the audacity to do something risky; it's about having the courage to do what is right. It's not about running in the dark; it's about walking in the light. It's not about believing what people say about God; it's about believing what God says about us.

The gospel of John uses the word *believe* more than any other book in the Bible. In fact, John claims to have been sent from God as a witness to testify so that all may believe (1:7).

Belief is generally not thought of as work, but it is. Jesus said, "The work of God is to believe in the one he has sent" (6:29). Belief doesn't pour out of heaven and into our heads; it requires mental effort. But people want God to do all the work. Even those who lived near Jesus and witnessed His miracles asked for more "proof." Comparing Jesus to Moses, they asked, "What miraculous sign then will you give that we may see it and believe you? . . . Our forefathers ate the manna in the desert; as it is written, 'He gave them bread from heaven to eat'" (John 6:30–31).

The startling thing about their request is that just the day before Jesus had indeed given them bread. He had fed five thousand of them with the bread from one boy's lunch!

Resisting the urge to say, "What about the bread I fed you yesterday!?" Jesus said instead, "I am the bread of life."

The reasons people give for not believing God often boil down to something they want God to do to prove Himself. Comedian Woody Allen has been quoted as saying, "If only God would give me some clear sign! Like making a large deposit in my name at a Swiss bank."

In making personal "to do" lists for God, however, we miss seeing the countless things He has already done. When we wait in doubt and disappointment for God to do the one thing we demand of Him, we miss seeing everything God is doing and has already done.

BEYOND BELIEF

Whenever I hear the song "God Is on Our Side," I feel uneasy. I think of some of the dastardly things that have been done by people boldly making this claim, and I fear that some people today are making it without the serious self-examination that must precede such a declaration. For God is only on the side of those who are on His side—those who desire to know His mind and do His will—not those who insist on convincing God that their way of doing things is right.

Abraham Lincoln said, "I do not boast that God is on my side; I humbly pray that I am on God's side." Lincoln was expressing the idea set forth by Azariah to King Asa of Judah. After the Spirit of God came upon him, Azariah said, "The LORD is with you while you are with him. If you seek him, he will be found by you; but if you forsake him, he will forsake you" (2 Chronicles 15:2).

A friend once asked me, "Do you think Judas knew that he was wrong?" I don't think he did, at least not until after the deed was done. Some of history's most despotic acts have been done by people convinced that their actions would make the world a better place. Many have even been done by those claiming to know God and be acting on His behalf. Many tragic lessons of history have been taught by those who believed with all of their heart that they were right when they were not.

One of my favorite *Peanuts* comic strips features Charlie Brown saying to Snoopy, "I hear you're writing a book on theology. I hope you have a good title." Snoopy responds, "I have the perfect title: *Has It Ever Occurred to You That You Might Be Wrong?*"

Snoopy's title reminds us that no one is always right, and Paul's teaching reminds us that when we're wrong we need to quickly "repent, turn to God, and do works befitting repentance" (Acts 26:20 NKJV).

> A spinning coin cannot spin forever, nor can our minds remain undecided forever, since not to decide is itself a decision. . . . Either we conform our desires to the truth, or we conform the truth to our desires.
>
> OS GUINNESS

The Greek word translated "repent" is *metanoia*, which means "change your mind." As Paul indicated, it does not mean just turning our heads toward God, nodding in polite agreement, and continuing on our own way. When we turn our thoughts toward God—when we truly agree with Him about what is good—our behavior will follow. Like a car, we go in the direction we're pointed.

I ONCE HAD A PICTURE COME TO MIND that helped me understand my faulty way of seeing spiritual things. I was thinking about the way the world is and the way Satan wants me to see it. I saw myself in a small, slow-moving picture. My back was to the camera, and in front of me were prison bars from one edge of the frame to the other—left to right and top to bottom. My hands were grasping the bars, and my face was pressed between them. Beyond the bars was a beautiful field with lots of lush grass, a bubbling brook with a waterfall, and beautiful flowering trees and plants that waved slightly in a soft, warm breeze. But the bars kept me from enjoying any of it. I could only long for what I had no way of reaching. I would occasionally shake the bars or bang my head against them, but it was all a self-defeating attempt to get what I believed I could never have.

As I watched, the perspective started to change. Little by little the camera moved back, showing me more of the picture, and I was startled to see the wide-open space behind me. As the camera moved back further, I was even more startled to see that what was behind me was the beautiful place I was longing for. In front of me—beyond the bars—was a mirror reflecting it. As the camera moved back it also moved up, allowing me to see behind the mirror. And there was Satan, watching me through the one-way mirror, laughing because I had wasted so much time longing for his illusion. He knew all along that to get the real thing, all I had to do was turn around.

WHEN WE SET OUR MINDS ON THINGS ABOVE, we begin to see the world as God sees it, and we see people as God sees them. We come to know a God who is compassionate and gracious, slow to anger, and abounding in love and faithfulness (Exodus 34:6). And one day we'll be able to boast that we understand and know the Lord, who "exercises kindness, justice, and righteousness on earth" (Jeremiah 9:23–24).

I doubt if Mary the mother of Jesus would have made the decision to say yes to Gabriel had she not known God and the Scriptures. For Mary to submit herself to this life-altering call, she had to want God's will more than her own way. She had to believe that God loved her and wanted what was good for her. She had to know that God's purpose was better than her plan. She must have believed the writings of King Solomon: "In his heart a man plans his course, but the LORD determines his steps" (Proverbs 16:9) and "Many are the plans in a man's heart, but it is the LORD's purpose that prevails" (Proverbs 19:21).

Earlier I said that Satan planted within Eve the seed of desire for knowledge that God didn't want her to have. Eve's desire for knowledge was not bad, but the knowledge of evil was something that God wanted to keep to Himself. Creation was good, and He wanted to keep it that way. But Eve introduced evil into our lives and made it necessary for us to learn to distinguish good from evil.

We tend to think that evil should be obvious, but it's not. Evil masquerades as good. The book of Hebrews confirms that learning to tell the difference between the two requires more than a weekend seminar: "[S]olid food is for the mature, who by constant use have trained themselves to distinguish good from evil" (5:14).

Conscience is what hurts when all your other parts feel good.

UNKNOWN

God's desire to keep us from knowing evil wasn't just a hopeful plan for the past that died with Eve's disobedience; it is still God's will and part of His plan for the future. Writing to the church in Rome, Paul encouraged believers to return to the way God intended His people to be: "I want you to be wise about what is good, and innocent about what is evil" (Romans 16:19). This is a difficult assignment in a world that assaults us with images of evil parading as good, but it's one that we need to take seriously.

To discern good from evil, truth from lies, wholesome beauty from physical attractiveness, and genuine love from lonely neediness, we need to know what God says about these things. We need to have clear thinking and solid beliefs.

SCRIPTURE MEMORIALIZES TWO WOMEN for their thinking about God. One has become an example of doubt, the other of faith.

In Genesis, we read about Sarah, who laughed in disbelief after hearing an angel tell her husband that she was going to become a mother at an age when most women were already enjoying grandchildren or great-grandchildren:

> Your eyes are of little use
> if your mind is closed.
> **ARAB PROVERB**

> So Sarah laughed to herself as she thought, "After I am worn out and my master is old, will I now have this pleasure?" (Genesis 18:12)

Ironically, the wife of Abraham, the man known as "the father of faith" (Romans 4:12–13), is remembered for her doubt. She did not believe that God could fulfill a promise that experience told her was impossible.

In the Gospels, we read about another woman who, like Sarah, had waited for many years to have a desire satisfied. She, however, had kept her faith.

[S]he thought, "If I just touch his clothes, I will be healed." (Mark 5:28)

After twelve years of going from doctor to doctor, only to get sicker and poorer, this anonymous woman had the faith to believe that a rabbi could do for her what doctors could not. Instead of building her belief system on the foundation of her own disappointing experiences, she built it on her knowledge of the proclamations of ancient Jewish prophets who predicted that the Messiah would come with healing.

In her book *When Life and Beliefs Collide*, Carolyn Custis James confirms the importance of women having knowledge and theological understanding:

> [A] woman's interest in theology ought to be the first thing to catch a man's eye. A wife's theology should be what a husband prizes most about her. He may always enjoy her cooking and cherish her gentle ways, but in the intensity of battle, when adversity flattens him or he faces an insurmountable challenge, she is the soldier nearest him, and it is her theology that he will hear. A woman's theology suddenly matters when a man is facing a crisis and she is the only one around to offer encouragement (p. 51).

Whenever I speak at writers' or editors' conferences, I close with Philippians 4:8, one of my favorite verses. Turned into questions, this verse is a good way to test our thoughts: Are they true? Are they noble? Are they right? Are they pure? Are they lovely? Are they admirable?

When we ask ourselves these questions before opening our mouths or closing our minds, we are less likely to end up in trouble.

LOVING GOD WITH MY MIND means knowing the pattern of God's relationship with humanity: revelation, alienation, reconciliation. The pattern started with Creation, the Fall, and the giving of the Law. It continued in the Incarnation, the Crucifixion, and the Resurrection. And it keeps repeating itself in individual lives on a daily basis. God gives us life and breath, sunshine and rain, food and flowers, sunsets and sunrises, friends and family. Yet we are constantly enticed to pursue things that look nicer, smell sweeter, or promise something better.

When I love God with my mind, I agree with Him about what is good. I reconcile my thoughts to His until I think what He thinks. I agree with Him about the way things are, the way things should be, and what He wants me to do about it.

LOVING GOD WITH MY MIND answers the question "Why am I here?" *I am here to know God, to enjoy His company and the beauty of His creation, and to participate with Him in the most important work of all—redemption—as He patiently and lovingly brings all creation into reconciliation with Himself through increased knowledge of good rather than evil.*

REFLECTION QUESTIONS

- What thoughts guide me? Are they true? How do I know?
- Do I think my way to decisions or do whatever "feels" right?
- Do I think my way to decisions or follow whatever is popular?
- Does my thinking lead to solutions or problems?
- Am I more curious about good or evil? Am I more drawn to good or evil? Why?

WITH ALL MY *Strength*

Does It Matter What I Do?

On the morning of September 11, 2001, I had just finished reading the book of Esther for my devotions when I learned what was happening in New York City.

I didn't immediately see the relationship between the events that I'd just read about and those that I was watching on a small screen in my living room. But as the day and week progressed, I realized that the story of the Persian queen was like a 2500-year foreshadowing of the day we remember as 9/11.

The book of Esther tells the story of a young Jewish orphan who became queen of Persia, much of which is now Iraq and Iran. Not only did Esther live in the capitol of the world's most powerful nation; she also lived in the palace of the world's most powerful man, who also was one of history's most ruthless rulers. Esther was surrounded by wealth and luxury, but her privileged life was threatened when the cousin who raised her came to her with this troubling news: the fate of all the Jews living in exile in Persia depended on her willingness to risk her life by confronting her ruthless husband.

Imagine being in Esther's place. Would you risk losing your position of power, prestige, and comfort—perhaps even your life—to prevent a tragedy that seemed so unlikely to happen? Or would you rationalize that you could do more good for more people by staying alive than by risking death?

> Character cannot be developed in ease and quiet. Only through experience of trial and suffering can the soul be strengthened, vision cleared, ambition inspired, and success achieved.
>
> HELEN KELLER

Mordecai spoke forcefully to his cousin with words that may have sounded like this: "Listen, Esther, don't think for a minute that all of this good fortune has happened to you simply for your own pleasure. And don't be so foolish as to think that you will be spared just because you're living in the king's palace. If you don't save your people, God will, but no one will save you. And who knows, perhaps you've been put in this position for the sole purpose of doing what needs to be done today—saving the lives of your people."

After fasting and praying for three days, Esther accepted

the challenge and risked her life by appealing to the king, who then spared the lives of all the exiled Jews living in the Persian Empire.

As I listened to the stories of the phone calls made by people on United Airlines flight 93 that crashed in Pennsylvania, I thought, *That plane must have had some Esthers onboard.* They heard the call, recognized their duty, and risked their own lives to save others. And if God had people onboard that plane to thwart the enemy, He probably had people in other strategic places who could have stopped the evil of that day before it got so big and so ugly.

> Worry does not empty tomorrow of its sorrow. It empties today of its strength.
>
> CORRIE TEN BOOM

What if God had people stationed at various intersections along the way, who, for one reason or another, turned their heads, ignored the evidence, and refused to believe that anything bad would happen if they ignored "potential" evil. After all, how could they have known that taking the easy way on that day would lead to death for so many innocent people? How could they have known that ignoring a small suspicion would result in evil on a scale that the Western world seldom sees?

This leads to more personal questions: How much evil do I ignore in my own life because I refuse to believe that my anger, bad habit, or rebellion will ever hurt anyone, or will ever get so big that I can't control it? And how much evil do I ignore in other people because I am too much of a coward to try to stop it, or because I don't want anyone to dislike me, or because I don't want to be inconvenienced?

As I witnessed the unfolding drama of 9/11, I saw my own responsibility in a new way. As Mordecai said to Esther, "Don't think you're here simply for your own pleasure and enjoyment; you're here to stand against evil."

Whenever evil rears its ugly head, the world asks: Where is God?

Jesus told us where God is. Speaking to the disciples, He said: "Before long, the world will not see me anymore, but you will see me. Because I live, you also will live. On that day, you will realize that I am in my Father, and you are in me, and I am in you" (John 14:19–20).

> If I put my own good name before the other's highest good, then I know nothing of Calvary love.
> **AMY CARMICHAEL**

We can ignore the question. We can even join those who are asking it. Or we can say, "Here He is, living in me. In the power of Christ, I'm standing against evil. Will you join me?"

Weakness

EVERYTHING I NEVER WANTED TO KNOW

THE FIRST TIME I SAW THE DEAD SEA, I was startled by its beauty. It stretched before me like a sparkling array of diamonds strewn across a shimmering blue cloth. But the glittering beauty of the Dead Sea does not draw eager crystal collectors to its shoreline. The crystals that make the Dead Sea shimmer are salt. And while salt certainly has its place and purpose—it's great for enhancing the taste of food—we don't make jewelry out of it. No woman I know would be pleased to receive an engagement ring with a sodium chloride crystal substituting for a gemstone.

Why are women so fussy? Well, for one thing, salt today is common and cheap. Used as a symbol of love, that's what salt would say to a woman about her worth.

Diamonds on the other hand are not cheap. Finding them, recovering them, and cutting and polishing them is a long and costly process. When they are finally mounted in a setting of precious metal, they become a symbol used by millions to communicate enduring love and priceless value.

Diamonds are beautiful and valuable gemstones, but the process of becoming diamonds is anything but glamorous. They start as common carbon—black, dirty, and combustible. But through countless years of intense heat and high pressure deep within the earth, they become pure and strong. This makes them a good metaphor for spiritual strength, for God uses intense outside forces to rid us of our impurities and to perfect His strength in us.

When I started writing this section of the book, I was regaining physical strength after several months of chemotherapy and radiation. During that time, I learned more than I ever wanted to know about physical weakness. But as I regained physical strength, my emotional strength began to evaporate when an unexpected event caused me to question my purpose and value. A working relationship that I valued, with an organization that I thought valued me, was substantially reduced. Then a minor event plunged me into a state of emotional weakness that caught me off guard. After losing three feet of hair and being bald for nearly a year, one bad haircut should not be a big deal. But it was to me. I felt silly for being so weak. I know that hair grows. But knowledge was not enough. My reservoir of emotional strength had dried up. I pleaded with God to spare me from experiencing the same level of emotional weakness that I had suffered physically one year earlier.

I hate feeling weak! I prefer the illusion of strength to the reality of weakness. But the truth is, we all are weak and totally dependent on God. Some of us live in places where we have few reminders of this reality. We are able to structure our lives in ways that create an illusion of self-sufficiency. But sudden loss of health, income, employment, prestige, or a treasured relationship is a startling reminder of our complete dependence on God.

Despite many lessons, I have yet to learn that God's strength is made perfect in my weakness. The how and why remain a mystery to me. But Jesus set the example, and thus He is able "to sympathize with our weaknesses" (Hebrews 4:15). What seemed to be the ultimate act of weakness—submitting Himself to a humiliating death—turned out to be His act of greatest strength.

The fiery furnace of suffering—whether physical or emotional, whether persecution from without or humiliation from within—removes our impurities and makes us strong.

When I started studying the Greatest Commandment, I assumed that loving God with all my strength had to do with physical strength and was related to concepts like courage and obedience. But the word translated "might" or "strength" in Deuteronomy 6:5 is an adverb used to express "great degree or quantity: very, greatly, exceedingly, much." It signifies intensity. Like an exclamation point at the end of the command, it urges us to commit every desire of our heart, every breath of our soul, every thought and attitude of our mind to the praise and glory of God.

Whatever you do,
work at it with all your heart,
as working for the Lord.
COLOSSIANS 3:23

Certainty

THE STRENGTH OF
My HEART

AT THE MILITARY MUSEUM IN ISTANBUL, visitors can hear some of the earliest military music. The Ottomans claimed to be the first to send troops off to war accompanied by musicians. However, the Ottoman Empire didn't begin until 1299, and the biblical record indicates that Jehoshophat, king of Judah, used music in battle during his reign thousands of years earlier (c.873–849 B.C.).

Jehoshophat knew that his army was powerless to defend his small kingdom against the vast army coming from Edom to attack them, so he gathered the people together at the temple of the Lord and pleaded with God for help. He ended his prayer with these words: "We do not know what to do, but our eyes are upon you" (2 Chronicles 20:12).

By acknowledging his own weakness, Jehoshophat made room for God's strength.

God answered quickly but not directly. He sent his response by way of Jahaziel the priest, a descendant of Asaph, a songwriter and worship leader. Through Jahaziel, the Lord said to Jehoshophat, "Do not be afraid or discouraged . . . the battle is not yours, but God's" (v. 15).

> And whatever you do, whether in word or deed, do it all in the name of the Lord Jesus, giving thanks to God the Father through him.
>
> COLOSSIANS 3:17

Jehoshaphat's response was two-fold. First, he worshiped (v. 19). Second, he appointed worship singers to lead the army. Before the battle even began, the service of praise and thanksgiving started. As they sang "Give thanks to the LORD, for his love endures forever," the Lord set ambushes against the invaders, and they were defeated.

The difference between the Ottomans and the people of Judah is notable. Whereas the Ottomans used music to lift the spirits of soldiers, the Israelites used music to lift praise to the Lord.

The purpose of praise is not to energize or empower ourselves, but to express our confidence in God's love and power. However, the by-product of praise is that it does energize us. Praise proclaims our steadfast trust in God's good intentions and in His ability to right the world's wrongs even when it appears as if His side is losing. When we affirm this truth with our mouths, we hear it with our ears, and it starts a spiritual process that is like the physical process of blood circulating in our veins. When we praise God for His strength, we are strengthened. By acknowledging God's strength, we realize our strength in Him.

> Be joyful always; pray continually; give thanks in all circumstances, for this is God's will for you in Christ Jesus.
> 1 THESSALONIANS 5:16–18

THE PHENOMENON SURROUNDING the publication of the book *The Prayer of Jabez* was a curiosity to me. How could so much be made of such a short passage of Scripture when so much of the Bible presents a contrasting view? Jabez asked God for several things, culminating in a request that he be spared from pain (1 Chronicles 4:10). The story has a seemingly happy ending, for the verse ends with these words: "And God granted his request." But what did Jabez do with his pain-free life? We don't know. All we know is that God didn't consider it worth writing about. In the margin of my Bible I wrote: "And Jabez was never heard from again."

Like Jabez, I want to be spared from pain. But in case after case throughout Scripture, God did His most remarkable work through people tested and tried and strengthened in the heat and pressure of pain and persecution. I am not suggesting that it is wrong to pray for relief from pain. Even Jesus prayed that God might have a Plan B in mind that would allow Him to avoid crucifixion. But in submitting to the will of His Father, He made it possible for you and me to avoid eternal suffering.

Several people I know are suffering unimaginable losses. One lost the ability to perform routine tasks as the result of treatment for a brain tumor. One lost all mobility in an accident. Others have lost children. But their testimonies of praise prove that God's strength is being made perfect in their weakness. Even though they never would have chosen their circumstances, they do not doubt that God loves them. They remain confident that He wants what is good *for* them and wants to accomplish good *through* them. They are learning to "delight in weaknesses, in insults, in hardships, in persecutions, in difficulties. For when I am weak, then I am strong" (2 Corinthians 12:10). To "delight" in such overwhelming difficulties requires unshakeable faith in the loving character of God.

> I sometimes question my crusade to improve the image of pain. In a society that routinely portrays pain as the enemy, will anyone listen to a contrarian message extolling its virtues?
> PHILIP YANCEY

PRAISE IS NOT A NATURAL RESPONSE in times of fear and uncertainty. It is supernatural. The world witnessed this when two Michigan families became the focus of media attention after an accident killed five people from Taylor University and seriously injured one other. The family of Whitney Cerak grieved the loss of their daughter. The family of Laura VanRyn kept a bedside vigil while praying for their daughter's full recovery and watching for any signs that she was emerging from unconsciousness. Five weeks after the accident, in a reversal that stunned not only the families but the entire nation, Laura's family realized that the young woman they had been watching over was not their daughter, but her classmate Whitney. Although neither family spoke publicly until two years after the accident, they posted blogs that read like modern day psalms. When attacked by Satan's cruelest weapon, both families fought back with praise. Even their laments were punctuated with exclamations proclaiming their certainty of God's goodness. In their final blog, Laura's family quoted 1 Peter 1:3–7:

> Praise be to the God and Father of our Lord Jesus
> Christ! In his great mercy he has given us new
> birth into a living hope through the resurrection
> of Jesus Christ from the dead, and into an
> inheritance that can never perish, spoil or fade—

kept in heaven for you, who through faith are shielded by God's power until the coming of the salvation that is ready to be revealed in the last time. In this you greatly rejoice, though now for a little while you may have had to suffer grief in all kinds of trials. These have come so that your faith—of greater worth than gold, which perishes even though refined by fire—may be proved genuine and may result in praise, glory and honor when Jesus Christ is revealed.

Praise is exercise for the heart. We start when we are weak, and it makes us strong—strong in the Lord. The certainty that God's ways are better than ours is where strength of heart begins.

The LORD is my strength and my shield; my heart trusts in him, and I am helped. My heart leaps for joy and I will give thanks to him in song.

PSALM 28:7

Humility

THE STRENGTH OF
My SOUL

AFTER ATTENDING A FUNERAL at church, I headed across the street to the college where I was teaching freshman English. I was early, so I planned to sit in the café and study until time for class. I ordered a caramel latté and settled down to review my notes, making a point of sitting where I had a clear view of the clock.

While I was studying, a woman I had not seen for a long time came in. She too had been to the funeral so we talked about the service and our friend whose husband had died in a plane crash. Then I told her about my class and how much I enjoyed the students. I kept checking the clock so I wouldn't be late. My class started at two o'clock, so I kept waiting for the minute hand to say "ten 'til." I checked several times, and the last time I looked, it said "fifteen after," so I figured I had at least another thirty minutes before heading to class.

As we were talking, one of my students walked up to our table. I smiled at him and introduced him to my friend. Then he handed me a stack of papers.

"What's this?" I asked.

"Our assignments that were due today," he said.

"Why are you giving them to me now?" I asked.

"Because you never came to class," he explained.

"What do you mean? I'm right here." I looked at the clock again. The minute hand said twenty after. To me that meant I had forty minutes before class started.

> It is often (always?) our mistakes that get us going on the spiritual journey. Error is turned into pilgrimage.
>
> ALAN JONES

"Class starts at two," he said. "It's twenty after."

I realized then that I had been so focused on the minute hand that I was not seeing the hour hand.

"Why didn't someone come and get me?" I asked.

"We didn't know you were here until just about everyone had left," he said.

I wanted to believe him because I wanted to think the best about the young Christian students preparing to take my place in the ranks of Christendom when my time expires.

But I remembered myself at their age, so I had some sizeable doubts. Besides, the café where I was sitting was located below a balcony just outside my classroom, and I suspected that my students had been watching from above and waiting for the college-mandated twenty minutes to pass so they could legitimately consider the class canceled and not be marked absent.

Some of the words we'd been discussing and writing about came to mind. One of the words was *anonymity.* I definitely did not want my name attached to this incident. Even though I could not keep the secret from my students, I immediately started plotting a way to keep it from my husband. Jay understands how things like clocks and numbers work and is somehow able to make them work for him. With me, they are more belligerent, and I always feel like a failure when I can't get them to cooperate.

Failure was another word we had discussed. Just a week earlier, I had handed back some papers with rather disappointing grades. After letting the shock set in, I gave my students a cheerful little speech about how we often learn more from our failure than from our success. My plan, however, was for them to learn from their own

Jesus Christ can afford to be misunderstood; we cannot. Our weakness lies in always wanting to vindicate ourselves.
OSWALD CHAMBERS

failure, not from mine. I prefer not to have God use me as a bad example.

To avoid telling Jay this new story about my inability to live in real time, I decided that I would adopt the "don't ask, don't tell" policy. That way I wouldn't have to lie, and he wouldn't have to know. It seemed like a win-win solution. But on Saturday, as we drove home from a choir workshop, Jay suddenly asked, "How did your class go on Friday?" Without a moment's hesitation I said, "Fine."

I'm not sure which surprised me more: How quickly the lie came to my lips or how quickly the rationalization came to my mind. *It wasn't really a lie,* I told myself. *The class really did "go" well. The whole class "went" right out the door.*

As soon as the word escaped from my mouth it started ringing in my ears. Even though I had redefined the word lie to absolve myself of guilt, I knew I was still guilty of deceit.

I put off the confession until the next morning on our way to church. As we neared the place where I had told the lie, I finally spoke the truth. Our marriage survived, but my ego spent quite some time in recovery.

My reason for telling this story is to

> We all have a lurking desire to be exhibitions for God, to be put, as it were, in His show room. Jesus does not want us to be specimens. He wants us to be so taken up with Him that we never think about ourselves, and the only impression left on others by our life is that Jesus Christ is having unhindered way.
>
> OSWALD CHAMBERS

illustrate how difficult confession is. If it's so hard to confess such a small thing because it's personally humiliating, the likelihood that I will have the courage to admit when I am wrong about something of more consequence is remote.

I prefer to have God use my strength rather than my weakness, but that's not His preference. He wants to show His strength, not mine, and His strength is impossible to see when I keep trying to impress others with mine.

You give me your shield of victory, and your right hand sustains me; you stoop down to make me great.
PSALM 18:35

OVER THE CENTURIES, the entrance to Bethlehem's Church of the Nativity has twice been made smaller. The purpose in the last case was to keep marauders from entering the basilica on horseback. The entrance now is referred to as the Door of Humility because visitors must bend down to enter.

As we age, bending our knees becomes increasingly difficult and painful—both physically and spiritually. In the physical realm, some people undergo knee replacement surgery. To avoid years of increasing pain and debilitating joint damage, they endure several weeks of agony.

Like physical knees, spiritual knees become stiff over time. Years of stubborn pride and self-centeredness make us inflexible, and it becomes increasingly difficult and painful for us to humble ourselves. Seduced by false feelings of importance when others submit to us, we never learn that true importance comes from submitting ourselves to God and others (Ephesians 5:21; 1 Peter 5:5).

The Door of Humility at the Church of the Nativity reminds us that we all need new knees—knees that will bend. The replacement procedure is painful, but it's the only way anyone can enter the presence of God.

In church we sometimes sing "Holy Is the Lord" by Chris Tomlin. When we get to the words "We stand and lift up our hands for the joy of the Lord is our strength," several people stand up. By the time we get to the next phrase, the whole congregation is standing. But the next phrase is "We bow down and worship Him now." I have yet to see anyone bow down when we sing those words. But the truth is, none of us can stand without first bowing down.

> The LORD upholds all those who fall and lifts up all who are bowed down.
> PSALM 145:14

Bowing is difficult because it's associated with submission. But imagine what a difference it would make if, in church, we had the strength to bow down and submit ourselves to God and one another, and, in the world, we had the courage to stand up for Christ.

The only real strength any of us have is God's. And the

only official act of strength God asks that we perform on our own is to humble ourselves. Doing so is the solution to the basic human condition inherited from Adam and Eve. The book of Genesis states that we have fallen and we can't get up. The rest of Scripture outlines the simple but difficult solution: The only way to get up is to bow down!

Who falls for love of God
will rise a star.
BEN JONSON

Unity

THE STRENGTH OF
MY MIND

I ONCE DECORATED a notebook with definitions of the words *opinion, preference, belief,* and *conviction* to remind myself that they are not synonyms. My certainty is misplaced when I am overconfident of my own opinions. Nevertheless, I find it difficult to resist the temptation to elevate my opinions and preferences to the level of beliefs and convictions.

Scripture says that we need to subjugate even our beliefs and convictions to the law of love (Romans 13:8, 10; Galatians 5:14; James 2:8), for love transcends all other laws and leads to peace and mutual edification. Whenever opinions and preferences become more important to us than what God says is true, important, and valuable to Him, we have made idols out of them, and this results in conflict and division.

Idolatry is the most serious offense in the Bible because it violates the first and most important command: "You shall have no other gods before me" (Exodus 20:3). An idol is more than a carved or forged image. It's a symbol of everything that the god stands for (or in most cases "falls for").

The Bible is filled with stories of people who go to all kinds of trouble to create and care for gods that are worse than helpless—they're needy! False gods fall over and have to be set upright. They have to be carried from place to place (or washed or cleaned or put away; or, in the case of opinions and preferences, defended). They are a burden. But people would rather cater to the gods they create than bow down to the One who created them. They work tirelessly to appease false gods but refuse to do the one thing that will make them acceptable to the one true God: bow down.

Few people are willing to set aside personal preferences for the sake of peace and mutual edification, but that's what Paul encouraged believers in Corinth to do:

If you think you are standing firm, be careful that you don't fall! No temptation has seized you except what is common to man. And God . . . will not let you be tempted beyond what you can bear . . . so that you can stand up under it.

1 CORINTHIANS 10:11–13

I appeal to you, brothers, in the name of our Lord Jesus Christ, that all of you agree with one another so that there may be no divisions among you and that you may be perfectly united in mind and thought. (1 Corinthians 1:10)

WHEN OUR CHOIR DIRECTOR raised his baton to begin the song, we lowered our heads to focus on our music. He established the tempo, keeping the rhythm with his arms. We tried to sing the song perfectly, paying close attention to each note as we moved through the score.

If you have any encouragement from being united with Christ, if any comfort from his love, if any fellowship with the Spirit, if any tenderness and compassion, then make my joy complete by being like-minded, having the same love, being one in spirit and purpose.
PHILIPPIANS 2:1–2

After several bars, the director's arms began moving more emphatically. We looked more closely at our music, trying even harder to get the words and notes right. But he seemed increasingly displeased.

What was evident to the choir director slowly became obvious to the rest of us. We were singing the right notes, but we weren't together. Each of us had our own tempo—all slightly different from his. Technically speaking the gap was small—a mere split second—but artistically it was a gaping hole.

Realizing that no amount of frantic waving was going to get us together, the director dropped his arms to his sides and stood motionless. We continued to sing, however, our heads buried in our music, unaware that he had stopped. Our eyes kept moving methodically from one note to the next, but the more we struggled to get ourselves together, the further apart we moved.

One by one our voices went silent as we realized that we were singing without a conductor. When at last the rehearsal room was quiet, he spoke. "You've got to get your noses out of your books," he pleaded. "We've been rehearsing this music for weeks. You know it better than you think you do. You've got to watch me. I know which parts give you trouble. Trust me to give you the cues. When you keep your noses in the book, you sing like robots. You have no life, no enthusiasm, no passion. You can't get energy out of the book; you've got to get it from me."

> Without music, life is a journey through a desert that has not ever heard the rumor of God. In music's sweet harmony, I had all the proof I needed of a God who held the earth together between the staffs, where the heavens lay. Here, he marked all the lines and spaces with notes so perfect that they praised all his creating with their beauty.
>
> PAT CONROY

He was right, of course. The music improved significantly when we trusted him to lead us.

This experience led me to wonder if something similar is going on in heaven. Could it be that Jesus is waiting for us to realize what a confused mess we're in, waiting for us to stop our futile striving long enough to hear Him say, "You've studied my Word for years. You know it better than you think you do. It's time to look at Me. I know there's security in having words in front of you, but you've got the Word inside you. Looking at words on a page may keep you from making a few mistakes, but it won't keep you together. Only I can do that—and only if you keep your eyes on Me. Keeping your nose in the book will help you get the words right, but there won't be any energy or power because you won't be together. Words convey truth, but only I can give life."

I'm not suggesting that we ought not bury our noses in the Book. Certainly there is a time for that. But there is also a time for looking unto Jesus, the author and perfecter of our faith (Hebrews 12:2). God said that He would put His laws in our hearts and minds (Jeremiah 31:33; Hebrews 10:16). When His Word is part of us, it becomes obvious to others in the way we live.

The evidence that we are living "right," Jesus said, is our unity. On the night He was betrayed, He prayed for Himself, for His disciples, and for us. His prayer for those who would believe in Him through the message of the disciples included this request:

I pray . . . that all of them may be one, Father, just as you are in me and I am in you. May they also be in us so that the world may believe that you have sent me. I have given them the glory that you gave me, that they may be one as we are one: I in them and you in me. May they be brought to complete unity to let the world know that you sent me and have loved them even as you have loved me. (John 17:21–23)

And over all these virtues put on love, which binds them all together in perfect unity.

COLOSSIANS 3:14

Good musicians don't need to hold up their music to prove they're singing correctly; their performance is proof enough. And Christians don't need an assortment of all-occasion Bible verses to prove we are right; our lives should be proof enough.

When believers are united in the love of Christ, the strength of the church will be unmistakable to the world.

Integrity

THE STRENGTH OF
My LIFE

ONE DAY IN COLLEGE, my English professor opened class with this peculiar prayer:

> Humpty Dumpty sat on a wall
> Humpty Dumpty had a great fall
> All the king's horses and all the king's men
> Couldn't put Humpty together again.

We were surprised to hear our Shakespeare professor praying a nursery rhyme, but he ended with these words: "Thank you, Lord, that you can do what kings cannot—you can put Humpty Dumpty together again."

Thankfully, he was right, for we are all Humpty Dumptys. None of the bonding agents the world produces can mend our brokenness. No matter how much self-repair we do, we remain broken and unable to pull ourselves together.

The most important commandment, Jesus said, is this: "Hear, O Israel: the Lord our God, the Lord is one. Love the Lord your God with all your heart and with all your soul and with all your mind and with all your strength" (Mark 12:30–31). The first part of the command says that God is one, but the second part indicates that we are not one; we are in parts. The aspects of our being—heart, soul, mind, and flesh—were broken apart when Adam and Eve plunged headlong into sin. Since that moment, ominously referred to as "The Fall," humanity has been in pieces, and all of us have been making vain attempts to repair ourselves. God's plan of redemption is to put us back together again. Apart from Him, it cannot be done.

We sometimes use the word "together" to refer to someone who appears perfect. When we say, "She's so 'together,'" we mean that her clothing and accessories are perfectly coordinated and that her family and career are perfectly balanced. God's idea is different. He intends that our hearts, souls, minds, and bodies all be fitted together in Him. In other words, He wants us to have integrity.

The word *integrity* comes from the word *integer*, which means "whole" or "complete." A synonym in Scripture is "perfect."

When Jesus said "you are to be perfect as your heavenly Father is perfect," He used the Greek word *teleios*, which also means complete. Jesus wants to make us whole by making us one with Him, one with ourselves, and one with others.

MANY OF US HAVE friends or family members who once claimed to be Christians but later abandoned the faith.

How many people have walked away from faith because their systematic theology proved unable to answer the deep longings and questions of the soul? What we need here, truly, is faith in a Being, not a list of ideas.
DONALD MILLER

When we consider the factors involved in their decision, we realize that in many cases the "god" they walked away from was not the one, true God, but a partial god, and a god who is not whole is easy to dismiss.

Those raised in austere, legalistic environments easily walk away from a god who is always angry and demanding. Those who were taught that god is more of an intellectual idea than a living, loving being find other "ideas" more intriguing and satisfying. Those who have a "best buddy" god, leave him when human buddies provide companionship more to their liking, perhaps by endorsing their sin or weaknesses. Those whose god is only a reflection of themselves are fascinated for a time, but only a narcissist can have a long-lasting relationship with his or her own image.

Whenever select aspects of the one, true God are emphasized and others excluded, we end up with an incomplete god who is not worthy of worship. As beings who are created in His image, we need to beware of the temptation to worship an image of God that most closely resembles ourselves. Emotional people can be tempted to worship an emotional god. Intellectual people can be tempted to worship an intellectual god. Socially minded people can be tempted to worship a "do-good" god. God is all of those things and more, but He is not any one of them alone.

> And let endurance have its perfect result, so that you may be perfect and complete, lacking in nothing.
>
> JAMES 1:4 NASB

AT MY ANNUAL PHYSICAL EXAM, my doctor asked his usual probing question. "Any problems with your health this year?"

In the past I had been able to say, "No, just colds and stuff." But that year I had my list ready.

"Well, I've been slowing down a lot," I said. "And when I sit on the floor, I have a hard time getting up again."

"That's pretty normal for your age," he said. "It's just going to get worse. If there's anything you want to do, do it now."

"Thanks," I said. "I'll call you the next time I need encouragement."

He smiled and then continued his speech. "Exercise would help. At your age it's more important than ever to maintain motion. If you don't exercise your muscles, your joints have to do all the heavy work, and that causes a lot of stress. Anything else bothering you?"

"Yes. I'm always cold and tired and I've been gaining weight. Are there some vitamins or something I could take to speed up my metabolism?"

"No. You just need more exercise. Exercise develops muscle, and muscle burns more calories than fat. Anything else?"

"Yes. Do you know anything about shoulders?" I wasn't trying to insult him, but he's a gynecologist, and I didn't know how much time he'd spent studying the skeletal system.

"I broke mine a couple years ago," he said. "I learned something then. What's your problem?"

"I think it's out of joint or something. I'm wondering if I should go to a chiropractor."

I demonstrated my limited range of motion, and then he tugged and pulled my arm into positions that caused my eyes to squeeze shut in pain.

Finally he announced his diagnosis. "Tendonitis," he said. "You're going to have to work it out. It'll be very painful, but if you don't do it your shoulder will freeze up. Then you'll have to go to physical therapy, which will be even more painful—and costly."

While demonstrating what I needed to do, he explained, "Poke around until you find the place that hurts the most. That's the injured tendon. Massage it as hard as you can as you move your arm. It will feel like a knife going through your shoulder, but that's what it will take to loosen it up."

Later, as I did the painful shoulder exercises, I recalled these words: "Exercise yourself toward godliness, for bodily discipline is only of little profit, but godliness is profitable for all things, since it holds promise for the present life and also for the life to come" (1 Timothy 4:7 NKJV; 4:8 NASB).

Finally, be strong in the Lord and in his mighty power.
EPHESIANS 6:10

When it comes to physical health, we believe experts who tell us that exercise is important. Yet we are slow to believe that spiritual exercise is essential for spiritual health. Those who join a sports team expect to put in long hours of practice, and no right-minded coach would put a player into a game who doesn't know the rules. Why, then, do we expect God to use us for something great even though we live on the spiritual equivalent of junk food, read the Bible as if it were a good luck charm, and seldom attempt to practice what it says we're to do? We know that being a spectator will not get us into any sports hall of fame. Yet we sit on the spiritual sidelines and expect to become strong in the Lord. To accomplish the mighty things God wants to do in and through us, we have to do difficult things through Him.

Physical and spiritual exercise have this in common: both are painful. Both require us to do something that one part of our body does not want to do. In the case of physical exercise, our flesh says to our mind: "This hurts. If you really loved me, you wouldn't make me do it." The mind knows that the opposite is true: Demanding that the flesh do something painful is actually *proof* of love. In order for our bodies to work properly, our minds and hearts must be in agreement as to what is good, and our bodies must submit.

> If one part suffers, every part suffers with it; if one part is honored, every part rejoices with it.
>
> I CORINTHIANS 12:26

In the spiritual realm, because of our broken condition, every part looks out for its own self-interest and has the ability to give the other parts bad advice. Faulty thinking about self-image may take control and refuse our body the food it needs to maintain health. Faulty desires may take control and refuse to give up a relationship that our mind knows is bad for us. Or physical cravings may take control and refuse to give up a substance or behavior that is destructive.

Satan has an alarming ability to exploit our weaknesses by exaggerating our strengths. He convinces us that we are good, not God; that our way is right, not God's; that our thoughts are reasonable, not God's; that our feelings are valid, not God's. Exercise in godliness helps us combat these deadly deceptions.

In the realm of physical fitness, expert Greg Landry gives this advice: "Look for the 'hard' way to do things." This is like the spiritual advice Jesus gave when He said we are to love our enemies and do good to those who hate us (Luke 6:27). Being kind to those who are nice requires little spiritual strength—even pagans can do it, Jesus said. But being kind to our enemies requires spiritual training equivalent to that of an Olympic athlete. We can't do it without spiritual coaching, much practice, and many bumps and bruises.

Spiritual exercise, like its physical counterpart, requires that we do what feels bad in order to maintain good health. Like learning to hide the good that I do (Matthew 6:3–4) and reveal the bad (James 5:16). Like praising God when it seems as if I'm losing. Like humbling myself when I'm certain I should be exalted. Like giving up my pet preference for the sake of unity in my community of believers. Like putting others ahead of myself, forgiving those who hurt me, being kind to those who hate me, and not returning evil for evil.

One of the most difficult situations in which to exercise these virtues is when a once-loving relationship becomes spite-filled and vindictive. A spouse leaves us with a mound of debt and diminishing self-esteem. An adult child mocks our faith and belittles our values. An angry family member turns others in the family against us.

Those who say "sticks and stones may break my bones but names will never hurt me" must never have experienced the intense emotional pain of a failed dream, a broken relationship, or a personal attack. Snubs, slurs, slights, and insults make us feel as if we've been kicked in the stomach. They are as cruel as any physical blow, and they leave us feeling weak and helpless. The pain is even worse when it's inflicted by someone we love, or someone we thought loved us, or someone we trusted with our kindness or generosity.

King David experienced this kind of pain when his son Absalom led a rebellion to claim the throne. With his family divided and his army in disarray, David fled Jerusalem, weeping as he went. Along the way he encountered Shimei, a member of the family of Saul, the previous king. When Shimei shouted curses at David, David's men wanted to kill Shimei, but David stopped them. "Leave him alone," he said, "It may be that the LORD will see my distress and repay me with good for the cursing I am receiving today" (2 Samuel 16:11–12).

Most people are happy when someone offers to get vengeance on their behalf. But David realized that something bigger was going on. Although he did not stick around to suffer more abuse, he was aware that God might have a purpose for it and that good could come out of it if he refused to return evil for evil.

Goodness is the only investment which never fails.
HENRY DAVID THOREAU

Whenever we are being treated unjustly, it's good to remember that God may intend to repay us with good. In his letter to Christians living in Rome, the apostle Paul wrote, "Do not be overcome by evil, but overcome evil with good" (Romans 12:21). Goodness often seems like a wimpy weapon against the forces of evil, but many have used it with great effectiveness.

Ken Sande, founder and president of Peacemaker Ministries, gives this advice in his book *The Peacemaker*:

> When someone has wronged you, it is also helpful to remember that God is sovereign and loving. Therefore, when you are having a hard time forgiving that person, take time to note how God may be using the offense for good. Is this an unusual opportunity to glorify God? How can you serve others and help them grow in their

faith? What sins and weaknesses of yours are being exposed for the sake of your growth? What character qualities are you being challenged to exercise? When you perceive that the person who has wronged you is being used as an instrument in God's hand to help you mature, serve others, and glorify him, it may be easier for you to move ahead with forgiveness.

Everyday life in a broken world provides plenty of opportunities for exercise in godliness. But what is a good exercise routine? In his second letter, the apostle Peter gives an answer. He says, in fact, that if we do these things we will never fall (2 Peter 1:10):

> Make every effort to add to your faith goodness; and to goodness, knowledge; and to knowledge, self-control; and to self-control, perseverance; and to perseverance, godliness; and to godliness, brotherly kindness; and to brotherly kindness, love. (2 Peter 1:5–7)

The order of these attributes is not coincidental. There is a progression.

Goodness is the desire to do the right thing. It is first

because it marks the starting place of faith. Everything we do, good and bad, begins with desire. The desire to do what is right is the first step in our relationship with God.

Knowledge is the ability to discern what is right. It comes second because doing the right thing requires that we first figure out what right is.

Self-control is the resolve to do the right thing. It comes next because without steadfast determination, we will be tempted to change our minds when we find out that doing right is often very difficult.

Perseverance is the endurance to keep doing the right thing. It is self-control running the Boston Marathon. To persevere means that we continually control our passions and repeatedly act in accord with our knowledge of what ought to be done rather than give in to what we feel like doing.

Godliness is the goal of doing the right thing. It's an attitude we're to develop as our behavior improves. The danger that lurks in doing right is pride. When we begin moving toward spiritual maturity, the Enemy will try to make us believe that our improvement is due to our own efforts and for our own personal benefit. Godliness, however, is unselfishness. A godly person does the right thing not for selfish gain but so that the plan of God will be revealed and others might see a living example of how much better it is to follow God's way.

Brotherly kindness is the means of doing the right thing. It is the tangible expression of godliness revealed through acts of thoughtfulness, generosity, honesty, and concern.

Love is the highest motive for doing the right thing. It extends God's goodness to everyone, including the undeserving and even our enemies. We talk flippantly about loving God and loving one another, the commandment that Jesus says is the most important of all because it summarizes and incorporates all the others. But seen from this perspective, with a view of all the work that must precede genuine love, it becomes apparent that what we call love is often a pathetic substitute.

Although these attributes build on one another, we don't have to become perfect in one before working on the next. In *How Do You Live the Christian Life,* Mart De Haan wrote, "The seven steps . . . show us the logic and progression of real faith. They show us that God is not just looking for love or faith or knowledge. He's looking for all these characteristics as they combine to provide a complete, balanced, progressive Christian experience."

As we add these exercises to our routine, we "participate in the divine nature and escape the corruption in the world caused by evil desires" (2 Peter 1:4).

THE DIFFERENCE BETWEEN physical and spiritual exercise is that physical exercise stalls the inevitable—death by corruption—whereas through spiritual exercise we participate in the divine (incorruptible) nature and thus prepare for eternity.

We can't deny the evidence of social corruption and moral decay. Nor can we ignore the people desperate for an escape. God has provided the way out, and Peter has mapped the journey like a spiritual Mapquest. The way is narrow. At times, we may feel claustrophobic and be tempted to turn back. But following it is the only way to escape the corruption and to lead others out of it.

> The love of God in Christ Jesus is such that He can take the most unfit man—unfit to survive, unfit to fight, unfit to face moral issues—and make him not only fit to survive and to fight, but fit to face the biggest moral issues and the strongest power of Satan, and come off more than a conqueror.
>
> OSWALD CHAMBERS

I have a friend whose husband stole money from his employer. To avoid criminal prosecution, he agreed to pay it back. For several years, most of my friend's paycheck went to pay off the debt. Sadly, her husband continued his deceptive behavior and they eventually divorced. Due to state divorce laws, my friend was ordered to pay half the remaining debt. She couldn't afford to keep the family home, so she moved into an apartment. After several difficult job situations, she found a position that fit her interests and abilities. Through it all, she never spoke badly to her children about their father. Even when they blamed her for the breakup of their family, she refused to say or do anything to damage their relationship with their dad. Her ex-husband filed for bankruptcy to avoid paying his half of the debt. She is still paying her half. Her children now admire her for letting the truth reveal itself rather than revealing it to them in an attempt to vindicate herself. God is moving her toward wholeness.

I look at my friend with great admiration. She refused to return evil for evil, and God is now rewarding her with good. In one of his songs, David wrote, "Be still and know that I am God" (Psalm 46:10). My friend did the hard work of being still, and she has come to know God in an amazing new way through the work He has done on her behalf.

CHOOSING TO FOLLOW GOD will take us through some tight and uncomfortable places. The Bible is full of examples of people whom God purified and strengthened by pressing them through the narrow way of affliction.

This theme unfolded early for me one day. I logged onto my computer, clicked the link that connected me to one of my favorite Lake Michigan Web cams, and then went to work. But the unusual sight of a big barge trying to enter the channel to Lake Macatawa interrupted my concentration.

While I was watching, another sight grabbed my

attention. Waddling past the window in front of my desk went one, two, and then three chubby raccoons. One at a time the trio poked their heads into the sewer drain near the curb and squeezed their plump bodies into the place they call home.

Back at the channel, the barge was still trying to align itself between the two piers. I was getting the message. Big ship, narrow channel. Fat raccoons, narrow drain hole. It was time for me to investigate the subject of narrow.

I looked up the verse "small is the gate and narrow the road that leads to life, and only a few find it" (Matthew 7:14).

Previously I thought of the "narrow road that leads to life" as the "straight and narrow." Like a tightrope that I had to walk without falling, or like the channel leading from one body of water to another, it was difficult to navigate and allowed little if any room for error. However, the word *narrow* here means "pressed," "afflicted," or "distressed."

I realized then that the life God wants us to have comes not as a reward for walking the straight and narrow—as in strict adherence to a bunch of rules or laws—but as a result of going through the narrow "birth canal" of faith into new life as a child of God.

The road that leads to life takes us not along a tightrope stretched across the cavern of hell, but through tight places that squeeze us into the likeness of Christ (4:19).

IN A LETTER TO the church in Galatia, Paul indicated that the biggest spiritual danger is not "falling" into sin, but turning back when the pressure of righteousness starts to hurt.

Being hurt by a friend or loved one is bad enough, but what if God Himself takes away His hand of protection? That's what happened to Job. And not because he did something bad, but because he was good—so good in fact that God said of him: "There is no one on earth like him; he is blameless and upright, a man who fears God and shuns evil" (Job 1:8).

Job is the only person mentioned in the Bible whom God identified as having integrity. The Lord said to Satan, "[Job] still maintains his integrity, though you incited me against him to ruin him without any reason" (2:3).

In a short space of time, Job lost everything dear to him: his children were killed, his wealth disintegrated, his good name was tarnished, his closest friends suspected him of wrongdoing, and his wife considered him foolish for not turning against God.

Eventually even Job's health was taken from him. "The thing I greatly feared has come upon me," Job lamented (3:25). Job did indeed have *all of our* worst fears come upon him. His distress was so great that he pleaded, "May the day of my birth perish" (3:3). Job wanted God to erase all memory of his existence! He had enjoyed years of success and respect. Without those, he saw no purpose for living (3:20).

Job wanted to die and be forgotten, but instead God made sure his name and story would be remembered forever. Rather than give Job what he asked for, God gave future generations what they would need—an inside look at the spiritual battle between God and Satan. The result is a document of God's thoughts about suffering that has comforted countless people.

When Satan attacks us with his most powerful weapons, and the thing we greatly fear comes upon us, we know, thanks to Job, that God can use our suffering for good. Through it, He can strengthen us and perhaps future generations as well.

Suffering is the narrow way that leads to spiritual life and strength, for it is through suffering that we are prepared for eternal glory:

> And the God of all grace, who called you to his eternal glory in Christ, after you have suffered a little while, will himself restore you and make you strong, firm and steadfast. (1 Peter 5:10)

To some, faith is no more than an intense form of wishing. But real faith is work. It's our work. And our faith is

God's work. He is making our lives a work of art that will attract worshipers into His kingdom.

When we start with the mistaken belief that faith makes life easy, we waste energy and gain only frustration trying to make our faulty belief true. But once we concede that faith is hard work, we are free to use our energy in productive ways. Instead of wasting it on futile attempts to achieve an easy life, we can invest it in the productive pursuit of a *good* life. And the strength gained from living a good life eventually makes life easier as well because God's strength is perfected in us.

> This is what the Sovereign LORD, the Holy One of Israel, says: "In repentance and rest is your salvation, in quietness and trust is your strength."
> ISAIAH 30:15

FILLING OUR CALENDARS with charitable activities, or wearing ourselves out to accomplish items on a good-deeds checklist, is not what God had in mind when He told us to love Him with all our strength.

Rather, loving God with all our strength means calmly and quietly doing what God says is right in our day-to-day lives, trusting Him to use us in ways big or small, according to His choosing, to accomplish what's on His agenda, not ours. By doing right in little things that are difficult, we prepare for the time when God puts us into a situation that presents a big challenge. Loving God with all our strength means that we quickly repent of attitudes and actions that may seem right, but that keep us from being right with God.

I AM NOT THE MARTHA TYPE. God had something other than domestic skills on His mind when He formed me. But I know a few basics. I know that getting rid of stains requires scrubbing, and that eliminating wrinkles requires heat and pressure. The Bible uses this domestic metaphor when describing Christ's relationship to His bride, the church.

> The Lord is my light and my salvation—whom shall I fear? The Lord is the stronghold of my life— of whom shall I be afraid?
>
> PSALM 27:1

> Christ loved the church and gave himself up for her to make her holy, cleansing her by the washing with water through the word, and to present her to himself as a radiant church, without stain or wrinkle or any other blemish, but holy and blameless. (Ephesians 5:25–27)

The same things that produce the symbol of love, a diamond, also produce the object of love, the bride herself. Heat and pressure are required to make us holy and radiant. The purity formed in us through adversity is the strength of

Christ made perfect in us. To love God with all our strength is to find all our strength in Him.

Even the most perfectly cut and polished diamond has no beauty on its own. Without one essential component, a diamond looks much like other rocks. A diamond's beauty depends on light. A diamond in the dark is ordinary. Light makes all the difference.

LOVING GOD WITH ALL MY STRENGTH answers the question "What should I do?" *I should follow God wherever He leads. I won't know ahead of time where He will take me, but I know He will not lead me along the path of least resistance. He wants me to carry the light of His truth, goodness, and love into dark places where evil is causing chaos and confusion, and the strength I need cannot be gained apart from adversity.*

REFLECTION QUESTIONS

- What am I trying to accomplish?
- How do I get it done?
- Do I take the easy way or the right way?
- What am I uniquely qualified to do or in a unique position to accomplish?

Glorious God and loving
Father, may every desire, every
breath, every thought, and every
deed be for Your glory. Fit us for
heaven through our afflictions on earth.
May Your strength be formed in us through
the purifying forces You use in our lives. May
our purity enable the light of Your love to
radiate through us with such amazing beauty
that all the world is attracted to the splendor
of Your holiness. We are indebted to You for
all things, and to You all honor and glory
and power belong. Amen.

I STARTED THIS BOOK with an illustration about three characters from *The Wonderful Wizard of Oz* who represent three of the ways we're to love God. But what about Dorothy? Throughout the story, Dorothy wants only one thing—to go home. And isn't that what we all want, really?

We all long to find the place where we belong. If we grew up in a loving home, we try to re-create it or return to it. If we grew up in a not-so-loving home, we try to replace it with something better. We all want to find a family who loves us, a place where we can let down our guard without losing our safety—in other words, the place where we can rest.

The songwriter who was also ancient Israel's greatest king knew the location of that place. He wrote: "My soul finds rest in God alone; my salvation comes from him"

(Psalm 62:1). Augustine, in the opening of his *Confessions*, alluded to this psalm when he wrote:

> Can any praise be worthy of the Lord's majesty? How magnificent his strength! How inscrutable his wisdom! Man is one of your creatures, Lord, and his instinct is to praise you. He bears about him the mark of death, the sign of his own sin, to remind him that you thwart the proud. But still, since he is a part of your creation, he wishes to praise you. The thought of you stirs him so deeply that he cannot be content unless he praises you, because you made us for yourself and *our hearts find no peace until they rest in you*. (Book 1, italics added)

We all want to go home, but many of us spend our lives trying to find the place without realizing that we first need to find the person—the Father—the one who knows that home is where He is, the one who keeps calling us to come and enjoy His wonderful company, where we will be loved for all eternity.

And what do all the great words come to in the end, but that?—I love you—I am at rest with you—I have come home.

DOROTHY L. SAYERS

To him who is able to
keep you from falling and to
present you before his glorious
presence without fault and with great
joy—to the only God our Savior be
glory, majesty, power and authority,
through Jesus Christ our Lord, before
all ages, now and forevermore!

Amen.

JUDE 1:24–25

Acknowledgments

I AM INDEBTED to many people for their contributions to this book. Five friends began this journey with me by participating in a preliminary Bible study in which we started to explore the vast subject of loving God. They are Rika Diephouse, Donna Fagerstrom, Jill Miller, Ashley Ohman, and Judy Schreur.

To those who allowed me to tell their stories, especially my parents and my husband, I owe a special debt of gratitude. Their courage deserves recognition. I also acknowledge and thank those who allowed me to use their stories but who, for various reasons, preferred to remain anonymous.

I also want to acknowledge the generosity of those who allowed me to quote their work, especially Jill Herweyer, Jennifer Quartell, and Mary Timme.

I am indebted to Carol Holquist of Discovery House Publishers who had the courage to recommend to RBC Ministries that they allow me to develop some resources by and for women. The result was five Loving God booklets, which became the basis for this book.

And to my longtime friend, mentor, colleague, and now editor, Judith Markham, I say a special thank you. Judith has a rare ability to balance friendship and professionalism. I have long admired her gift for working with authors, and now that I am one of them I can confirm what many others already know: she is the best editor!

No book is the result of one person's effort. Each requires a team of talented people, so I want to acknowledge the work of the many others at Discovery House Publishers who had a part in the publishing of *Above All, Love*.

Note to the Reader

THE PUBLISHER INVITES YOU to share your response to the message of this book by writing Discovery House Publishers, P.O. Box 3566, Grand Rapids, MI 49501, U.S.A. or by calling 1-800-653-8333. For information about other Discovery House publications, contact us at the same address and phone number.